Macbeth:

COMPREHENSION, ANALYSIS, COMPOSITION

Authors

Barbara Bloy

Donna Tanzer

Peoples education

Your partner in student success™

www.PeoplesEducation.com

Martin Beller, *Consultant*

Executive Editor: Doug Falk
Supervising Copy Editor: Lee Laddy
Editorial Services: Carol Alexander
Senior Production Manager: Jason Grasso
Assistant Production Manager: Steven Genzano
Marketing Manager: Brian Moore

Cover image, Photos.com.

Your partner in student success™

ISBN   978-1-4138-4870-0

10   9   8   7   6   5   4   3   2

About the Authors

Barbara Bloy, Ph.D.

Barbara Bloy has 30 years of teaching experience that includes high school AP English Literature and college teaching. A former reader of the AP English Literature exam for the College Board, Dr. Bloy leads summer workshops for AP English teachers at the Taft Educational Center, Watertown CT. She has also conducted workshops at AP annual conferences and NCTE meetings. Dr. Bloy is the author of *English Literature—Close Reading and Analytic Writing*, published by Peoples Education.

Donna C. Tanzer, M.A.

A former teacher of high school AP English Literature, Donna C. Tanzer currently teaches writing and humanities for the Milwaukee Institute of Art and Design and a graduate education and children's literature course for Marian College of Fond du Lac, in Wisconsin. Ms. Tanzer has directed over 25 plays for the high school stage, including Shakespeare. An AP English exam reader for the College Board, she has published articles on education, drama, and poetry. Ms. Tanzer is also the co-author of Perrine's *Teacher's Advanced Placement Guide*, published by Cengage.

About the Consultant

Martin Beller, Ph.D.

Martin Beller has been a college and high school teacher for nearly twenty years, and now teaches English and Ethics at YES Preparatory Public School in Houston. He received his B.A. in English from C.W. Post College and his M.A. and Ph.D. from The Ohio State University, concentrating on Medieval and Renaissance literature. Dr. Beller has published articles and reviews on Shakespeare, Chaucer, Marlowe and Flaubert.

MACBETH

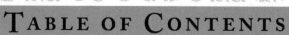

TABLE OF CONTENTS

Act 2

Act 3

Act 4

Act 5

To the Student

Macbeth may be the first of William Shakespeare's plays that you have read or seen, or perhaps you have already encountered Shakespearean drama in the classroom, on film, or at the theatre. You certainly know something about this writer, fact as well as fiction, and you may come to his play with feelings ranging from fear to anticipation of a difficult but worthwhile experience.

This guide is meant to allow you to experience *Macbeth* as a complex work of art, yes, but also as an accessible drama that can be understood on many levels. Passages from the play are presented in order, from a single line to longer speeches and excerpts of dialogue. Some of the techniques that you are asked to study in each passage are familiar and instantly recognizable: for example, Shakespeare's use of language in the dialogue of the witches. This book also introduces you to some sophisticated literary devices and the formal analysis of a line of poetry.

Two charts at the front of the guide will remind you of poetic and dramatic devices you have already studied; other terms may be new to you. One chart presents the terms in groups, so that you can review elements of verse form and rhetorical devices and note (with relief) that you have already worked with many of these when you studied novels and poems. The second chart presents each technique in alphabetical order and lists all places in which it is used. Each bolded literary term is defined or explained the first time it appears, while the glossary at the back of the guide lists terms alphabetically and defines the term fully.

You will be introduced to an example of each technique before you are asked to identify it and gauge its effect independently. The passages selected for close reading are introduced so that you will easily understand the context, especially since you will be working in the guide as you read each scene. Your text will have notes and summaries that provide explanations of unfamiliar language or other points of interest. The three exercises that call for responses to the passage will help you to prepare yourself for class discussions, quizzes, or in-class work in small groups or pairs. Individual work will sometimes be assigned by your teacher. These exercises may involve keeping lists of motifs, making entries in a reading journal, writing an analytic paragraph, or composing a formal analytic essay about a technique that you have followed throughout the act or the entire play. Depending on your grade level and how much experience you have had with poetry and with Shakespeare's plays, you may be instructed to skip passages or exercises that are too simple or too complex for the class—but they are there, in case you need extra practice or want to challenge yourself with difficult concepts.

After you have studied these passages, you are ready to bring Shakespeare's words to life in several *On Your Feet* activities. These segments are your opportunity to find what is moving and authentic in *Macbeth*—to take the words from the page and make them real. In order to better understand the effects of the language you are studying, you need to put yourself into the minds and bodies of the characters and understand their feelings and their conflicts. You need to *become* the characters by reading aloud and playing the scenes.

The operative word here is "play." As you experiment with voices and gestures, with emotion and nuance, you will increase your understanding of Shakespeare's craft and your appreciation of his artistry. If you have acting experience, you will be able to help your classmates as you develop and improve your acting skills. Working in pairs and groups will help those of you without a theatre background to ease into the process of acting. The word "play" also reminds you to enjoy yourself and have fun with this play of suspense, spectacle, and the supernatural.

MACBETH

LITERARY TERMS ARRANGED BY CATEGORY

CHARACTER
characterization
choral character
chorus
conflict
foil

CONTEXT
atmosphere
mood
setting

DICTION
ambiguity
connotation
disyllable
literal language
monosyllable
multisyllable
polysyllable
prose

DRAMA TERMS
aside
blocking
cast
cue
dialogue

downstage
improvisation
in character
offstage action
pacing
props (stage properties)
role
set
soliloquy
stage directions
subtext
upstage

FIGURATIVE LANGUAGE
apostrophe
metaphor
> grounds
> tenor
> vehicle

metonymy
personification
simile
symbol

IMAGERY
motif
scene-painting

METRICAL SUBSTITUTIONS

caesura
eleventh syllable
pyrrhic
rest
spondee
trochee

PLOT

backstory
foreshadowing
poetic justice

PROSODY

accent, stress
blank verse
end-stopped line
enjambed line
foot, feet
iamb (iambic)
iambic pentameter
line length
meter
pentameter
prose
prosody
rhythm
scan, scansion
trochee (trochaic)

RHETORICAL DEVICES

allusion
antithesis
apostrophe
equivocation
motif
paradox
parallelism
pun
repetition
rhetorical accent

RHYME

couplet
end rhyme
internal rhyme

SOUND DEVICES

alliteration
assonance
consonance
onomatopoeia

SYNTAX

inversion of word order
loose sentence
periodic sentence

TONE

hyperbole (overstatement)
irony
   dramatic
   verbal

MACBETH

LITERARY TERMS SCOPE AND SEQUENCE

Term	Introduction	Lessons/Exercises	On Your Feet
Accent / Stress	II, III, IV	37A	
Alliteration	IV, VI	22; 26A	VI, VIII
Allusion		26B	
Ambiguity		1; 5C; 7B; 18C; 22	
Antithesis		3, 3B; 5, 5A; 9B, C; 10, 10B; 11B; 13B; 14B; 24B	
Apostrophe		27	
Aside	I	8; 29	II
Assonance	IV	26A	
Atmosphere / Mood	I, IV	2B; 9B; 11B; 18B; 26B, C	IV, IX, XII
Backstory	I		
Blank verse	III	1	
Blocking			VII, IX
Caesura	III, VI		
Cast / casting	I		I, VII
Characterization	II	3C; 9C; 10, 10B, C; 11C; 20C; 21B	
Choral character	I	32; 36	
Choreography			IX
Chorus	I	32	
Conflict		9A	
Connotation		1; 3A; 8C; 9A, B; 31C	
Consonance	IV	26A	XIII
Couplet	III	24	
Cue	VII		VIII
Dialogue	I, II, V	17, 17B, C; 29B, C; 34; 38A	III, XI
Diction	VI, VII	4C; 9A; 10C; 11B, C; 13C; 16B; 18B; 19A; 20A; 22; 23B; 26B; 27B; 29A, B; 32B	
Disyllable	III	13C; 14C	

Term	Introduction	Lessons/Exercises	On Your Feet
Downstage	I	10	
Dramatic irony		21, 21C; 22; 24C	
Eleventh syllable	III		
End rhyme	IV		IX
End-stopped	III		
Enjambed line	III	1	
Equivocation		1, 1A, B; 7, 7C; 33B, C	X
Figurative language		1; 2C; 6; 27A; 33B	
Foil		17C; 20C; 23A	
Foot / Feet	III		
Foreshadowing		19, 19C; 22	
Grounds		6; 8C	
Hyperbole		36C	V
Iamb / Iambic	III, IV		
Iambic pentameter	III		
Imagery		2B, C; 9B; 11A, C; 18A; 22; 26B; 27, 27B	VI, IX
Improvisation			I, III
In character	VII		
Internal rhyme	IV		
Inversion of word order	VI		
Irony		21C; 25B; 26B; 33C	VIII
Line length	III		
Literal language		1; 2A; 6; 27A; 31A	
Loose sentence	VI		
Metaphor		1; 6; 8B, C; 10A; 12C; 13A; 19, 19B, C; 21A; 22; 25A; 31A; 34A; 36A, B, C; 37B	XI
Meter	III, IV, VI		IX
Metonymy		2C; 6	
Metrical substitutions	III	37B	
Monosyllable	III	13C; 14C; 20B; 22; 27C	VI
Mood / atmosphere	I, IV	2B; 9B; 11B; 18B; 26B, C	

Term	Introduction	Lessons/Exercises	On Your Feet
Motif	IV	1; 2, 2B, C; 6; 7B; 9B; 11A, C; 13B; 14C; 16A, C; 17; 18B; 19C; 25B; 29C; 34; 36C; 38C	
Multisyllable	III		
Offstage action		32	
Onomatopoeia		26A	VI
Pace / pacing	III	20B	VI, XII
Paradox		25C	
Parallelism	VI	4B, C; 5B; 14B; 15B; 22; 24B, C	
Pentameter	III		
Periodic sentence	VI	26C	
Personification		6; 13; 18A; 19B; 27A	
Poetic justice		34C	
Polysyllable		13C; 20B	
Props (stage properties)	I		VII, X
Prose	III	35, 35A	XII
Prosody	III		
Pun		1	
Pyrrhic	III		
Repetition	IV	1; 2B; 4B, C; 19A; 23B; 24C; 30A; 35A	IX, XIII
Rest	III		
Rhetorical accent	III		
Rhyme	III, IV, VI	24B	IX
Rhythm	III, IV		IX
Role	I	32	
Scansion / scan	III		
Scene-painting		27	
Set	I		
Setting	I		
Simile		6	
Soliloquy	I, II, V	10; 11C; 12; 18, 18B; 20; 23, 23B, C; 24	II, IV, V, XIII

Term	Introduction	Lessons/Exercises	On Your Feet
Sound devices	IV	14B; 26A; 27B; 37B	VI
Spondee	III		
Stage directions	I, VII		VIII
Stage properties (props)	I		VII, X
Stress / accent	II, III, IV	37A	
Subtext	I, III		III
Symbol		33	X
Syntax	VI, VII	1; 4B; 22; 26C; 32C	
Tenor		6; 8B	
Tone	II	1; 4C; 13C; 14C; 16B; 27B, C; 29B; 30A; 32B, C	IV, VII
Trochee	III, IV		
Upstage	I		
Vehicle		6; 8B, C; 10A; 34A; 36A	
Verbal irony		21, 21C	

MACBETH

I. Stage Conventions

All of Shakespeare's plays are divided into five acts and within each act a variable number of scenes. Except for explanatory words, these divisions are the only indications of the passage of time or a change of place. Theaters had no curtains, so only the entrance and exit of actors marked a scene's beginning or end. Arrivals and departures took place through the two doors **upstage** (the back wall, away from the audience). Somebody had to drag dead bodies off the stage or they would lie there during the next scene—or the rest of the play.

The plays were usually presented in an open-air theater in the afternoon, so there was no way to darken the stage to show that a scene happens at night. When scenes were acted indoors, in a palace or manor house, candles provided the only suggestion of daylight. In the absence of scenery, the **setting**, when and where each scene is set, often had to be indicated for the audience. For instance, Banquo's line "How far is't call'd to Forres?" (1.3) reveals that the heath on which Macbeth and Banquo encounter the witches is somewhere near that place. Similarly, Lady Macbeth speaks of Duncan coming "under my battlements," (1.5) showing that she is at home when she reads her husband's momentous letter.

Modern plays usually have **sets**, a fully furnished living room, for example, and **stage properties (props)**, such as full bookcases, vases of flowers, and wine glasses. These **props** provide a sense of place and social rank. Shakespeare's productions included elaborate costumes, but provided none of these other clues. In our modern theaters, elaborate lighting choices and recorded music offer time clues and establish the **mood** and **atmosphere**. Shakespeare had to create these elements with words alone.

Unlike moviemakers, Shakespeare did not have the option of using flashbacks to fill in the **backstory**, what has happened before the present action. Only through **dialogue**, discussion between the characters, does an audience learn who is who and what has taken place before the play's first words. Very few of the three thousand people in the audience at the Globe Theatre could see the actors' facial expressions. Their postures, movements, gestures, costumes, and, of course, their marvelous speeches, were the only guides to the **subtext,** how they felt. In some ways, this worked in the company's favor: it was less jarringly obvious that the **role,** or part, of Lady Macbeth was played by a boy whose voice had not yet deepened—as were all the female roles. Subterfuge would not have been necessary, however, as Elizabethan audiences expected that the cast of a play would consist solely of male actors.

The elaborate costumes did not identify historical periods as costumes do today. Rather, all of Shakespeare's plays were produced in what was "modern dress" to the Elizabethan audiences. Elizabethan dress clearly indicated rank and social status; only the titled and wealthy classes could afford sumptuous fabrics such as satin, velvet, and even corduroy. Brilliant colors, created by special fabric dyes, were also limited to the upper classes. Sumptuary laws, regulations limiting who could wear fine clothing, enforced this strict delineation as one means of maintaining the strict social structure of the time.

The wealthy sometimes donated their used clothing to theater companies, who considered these fine costumes their most valued possessions. The costumes worn in Shakespeare's plays reflected the hierarchy of Elizabethan clothing so that audiences could quickly recognize high status characters by their costumes. In contrast, peasants and poor characters wore wool in somber hues.

In these plays, words and actions are presented with little direct commentary or explanation. Several times in *Macbeth* it is necessary that a **choral character** explain something to another character in order to let us know what has been happening on the larger stage—the whole country of Scotland—or to reveal how the people feel about the Macbeths and their rule. A **choral character** is a minor character, rather like a **chorus** in an ancient Greek tragedy.

Shakespeare largely relied on **dialogue,** but he also depended on two conventions of the era. In an **aside,** a character speaks to the audience as though thinking aloud. In a **soliloquy,** the actor moves **downstage,** as close to the audience as he can get, and again speaks private thoughts aloud. The audience knows that these words convey the character's true feelings.

Many modern playwrights include specific **stage directions** in their scripts, instructions that describe the **set(s)** and costuming, the list of **props,** and details about makeup, lighting, and music. The director and technicians know what was intended by the author. **Stage directions** also help actors to interpret the characters they play. These directions may be useful to the actors as they:

- use their voices to convey meaning and emotion
- put the emphasis on certain words and syllables
- vary the speed at which they speak their lines, including when to pause and pick up cues
- decide which physical movements are appropriate to a line or speech
- decide which facial expressions suggest a character's thoughts and emotions

Precise description in modern **stage directions** helps make the **subtext** perfectly clear to the actor. But we have few directions from Shakespeare in the scripts that were published during his lifetime or shortly after his death. Modern directors and readers lack the advantage of Shakespeare's **casts**. Except for his last play, which does have some **stage directions**, Shakespeare was present at the rehearsals and performances. As the playwright, actor, and a shareholder of the company, he could tell his fellow actors what effect he was after. For instance, if the audience at the first performance laughed at something that wasn't supposed to be funny, he could rewrite lines.

A play on stage is already interpreted for us, but a reader has the opportunity to be the director and play all the **roles** in his or her imagination. The reader can unearth the clues embedded in the words, experimenting with how they might sound. Better yet, when readers work collaboratively on close reading and get on their feet to speak the words, the **subtext** becomes clear. The goal of this guide is to provide practice in how to discover the many clues and nuances present in the language. We must actively engage with the language in order to discover even the most basic elements of the play, such as where the action is **set** or how the characters attempt to solve their problems. What we gain from Shakespeare's superlative poetry includes a deeper understanding of ourselves.

II. Elizabethan English

Elision

Elision is the skipping of syllables to shorten words, with the omission indicated by an apostrophe. Examples in modern English include *I'd, he's, didn't*, etc. Some of Shakespeare's elisions also turn a subject and verb into a single word of one single syllable. Examples include:

'tis	it is
'twill	it will
thou'rt	thou art
thou'dst	thou wouldest

Many two-syllable words are elided, or slurred, into one, as modern English speakers do with *here's* for *here is* and *c'mere* for *come here*.

Examples from Shakespeare include:

do't	do it
ta'en	taken
ne'er	never
'twas	it was
o'the	of the
kind'st	kindest

Some elisions are not marked. Shakespeare assumed that the actors would elide some vowels and even whole syllables to keep the meter steady, the pattern of **stressed** and **unstressed** syllables that creates the flow of sound.

Sometimes entire words are omitted that we must supply. When King Duncan, listening to a report of the battle, hears that the enemy has fielded a fresh assault, he asks, "Dismayed this not our captains, Macbeth and Banquo?" The captain telling the news replies, "Yes, as sparrows eagles, or the hare the lion" (1.2.34–35). Given the context, that the news is good and that these brave heroes have won the war, we can supply the missing words: "Yes, they were as frightened as eagles would be by sparrows or lions would be by hares."

Expansion adds an extra syllable if one is needed for the **meter**. Shakespeare had the option, no longer available in modern English, to make the *–ed* at the end of a verb either nearly silent or a separate syllable. Sometimes he indicates that the ending is to be pronounced by using an accent grave: èd. But often, only the **metrical** pattern will tell you whether or not to pronounce the ending as a separate syllable. This line from 1.2.14 needs the extra syllable to satisfy the pattern of **stresses**: "But fortune on his damnèd quarry smiling. . ." Three lines later, 1.2.17, the **meter** would be disturbed if the ending of *brandished* were pronounced: "Disdaining fortune, with his brandished steel."

Pronouns

Pronouns were plentiful four hundred years ago. English had two forms of *you*, the second-person singular personal pronoun. Many other European languages have retained both forms, but because English has dropped *thou*, *thee*, *thy*, *thine*, and *thyself*, Shakespeare's usage can be confusing, both grammatically and in regard to social signals.

Thou is the nominative singular form, corresponding to *you*, used as the subject of a sentence: Thou hast.

Thee is the objective form of *you*, used as an object in the following examples:

I kiss *thee*	direct object
I give *thee* kisses	indirect object
I give kisses to *thee*	object of preposition

Thy is the possessive form.

Thine corresponds with *yours,* as in this example: the glory is *thine*. It is also used before an initial vowel (*thine* anger), as *mine* is used as the possessive *my* before a vowel (*mine* enemy).

Thyself, corresponding with *yourself*, is the reflexive or emphatic form (Thou *thyself* shall win the crown).

As in modern French, Spanish, Italian, and German usage, the choice of *you* or *thee* in Elizabethan English gave a clear social signal. *Thou* signals the intimacy between friends of equal social status. *Thou* might also indicate the superiority of the speaker over a social inferior. If used to address someone of a higher rank, *thou* is insulting and aggressive, conveying contempt. *You* is the more formal and distancing form of address, showing respect and courtesy to a social equal or to one of higher rank than the speaker.

To make things more confusing, the English language was changing in Shakespeare's time, and shortly afterward, *you* had entirely won out over *thou*. These usages are subtle, combining rules and the flux of social interplay. But often, if a speaker shifts from one to the other, it signals a change in attitude toward the person spoken to: "*Thou* hast" is appropriate from mother to child or wife to husband; "*You* have" displays anger directed at the child or husband. "*You* have" is appropriate from servant to master; "*Thou* hast" shows contempt toward one's master.

Here are some examples and exercises that demonstrate how the two forms of the pronoun are used according to custom, or deliberately misused to convey a social signal:

Example The king and a member of the nobility are using the pronouns according to the convention:

> DUNCAN   Noble Banquo,
> That hast no less deserved, nor must be known
> No less to have done so, let me enfold thee
> And hold thee to my heart.
> BANQUO   There if I grow
> The harvest is your own. (1.4.29–33)

Example The servant and his mistress are also following the convention:

> SERVANT The King comes here tonight.
> LADY MACBETH   Thou'rt mad to say it.
> Is not thy master with him, who, were't so,
> Would have informed for preparation?
> SERVANT So please you, it is true. (1.5.28-32)

Exercise A — As you read 1.3.43–66, when Banquo and Macbeth first meet the witches, notice their choice of second-person pronouns as well as which pronouns the witches choose when they speak to the thanes. What signal might Shakespeare's original audience pick up about how the men and the witches regard each other?

Exercise B — After her husband has followed his letter home, Lady Macbeth begins using the appropriate *thy*, but when she sees his reaction to her suggestion that Duncan shall never see another sunrise, she begins to use *you*. What do this change and the speech that follows show us about her emotions and basic **characterization**?

LADY MACBETH   Thy letters have transported me beyond

55   This ignorant present, and I feel now

The future in the instant.

MACBETH   My dearest love,

Duncan comes here tonight.

LADY MACBETH   And when goes hence?

MACBETH   Tomorrow, as he purposes.

LADY MACBETH   O never

Shall sun that morrow see.

60   Your face, my thane, is as a book where men

May read strange matters. To beguile the time,

Look like the time; bear welcome in your eye,

Your hand, your tongue; look like the innocent flower,

But be the serpent under't. He that's coming

65   Must be provided for, and you shall put

This night's great business into my dispatch,

Which shall to all our nights and days to come

Give solely sovereign sway and masterdom. (1.5.54-68)

Exercise C — The king is his guest, but Macbeth has left the dining table. Consider what the pronoun choice reveals about Lady Macbeth's **tone of voice** when she asks her husband, "Why have you left the chamber?" Macbeth replies, "Hath he asked for me?" The **tone** of her response is equally clear: "Know you not he has?" (1.7.29–30) Explain how she is feeling and what she wants to convey to her husband by her choice of pronouns.

Exercise D — A king uses the plural *we* to refer to himself in formal address. For example, King Duncan speaks thus to Lady Macbeth: "Fair and noble hostess, / We are your guest tonight" (1.6.24-25). Just before the following **dialogue**, Macbeth and Banquo have heard the witches' prophecies, and Macbeth has received a second title. He uses the royal *we* in speaking to Banquo, who has only one title. Consider the significance of the personal pronouns each character uses. How does Banquo now regard their relationship? How does Macbeth's last statement confirm your sense of why he uses the royal *we*?

BANQUO I dreamt last night of the three weird sisters.
To you they have showed some truth.

MACBETH   I think not of them;
20   Yet when we can entreat an hour to serve,
We would spend it in some words upon that business
If you would grant the time.

BANQUO   At your kind'st leisure.

MACBETH   If you shall cleave to my consent when 'tis,
It shall make honour for you. (2.1.18–24)

Exercise E — Banquo, in **soliloquy**, speaks to the absent Macbeth
after his coronation. What does his use of *thou* tell you about
his attitude toward a man who was a short time ago his equal in
nobility?

Thou hast it now: King, Cawdor, Glamis, all
As the weird women promised; and I fear
Thou played'st most foully for't. (3.1.1-3)

III. *Prosody*

Prosody, the study of versification, begins with the measuring
of poetry to determine its rhythmic meter, as well as its **line
length**. When we discuss **meter**, we use the term **foot**, meaning a
combination of syllables that constitutes the prevailing **meter** of a
poem. The vast majority of poems in English fall into **iambic** meter.
Each **iambic foot,** which consists of two syllables, has the **accent**
or **stress** occurring on the second syllable. **Iambs** are the natural
rhythm of the English language.

Shakespeare's plays use this neutral and flexible **meter** for
a wide range of tasks, from simply moving the plot forward, to
revealing the great complexity of a character's thought. The **line
length** that is easiest to speak in one breath and which doesn't
become singsong is ten syllables (five **iambic feet**): the **pentameter**
line. The plays are predominantly written in **iambic pentameter**
(five **feet** of **iambs**).

Rhyme, sound correspondences often found at the ends of
lines of verse, calls attention to itself, becoming monotonous in a
work as long as a play. To introduce variety, Shakespeare's **iambic**

pentameter is **unrhymed (blank verse)** except when he uses a **couplet,** two **rhyming** lines, to signal the end of a scene. The use of all other **meters** and **line lengths,** as well as ordinary **prose,** speech which is not in lines of verse, gave his original audience signals about the characters speaking them. You will see how these poetic devices work in the short, **rhyming** lines used by the witches in *Macbeth* and in the **prose** of Lady Macbeth's famous sleepwalking scene.

Blank Verse

In reading **blank verse,** punctuation must be followed just as carefully as the words themselves. Shakespeare understood the nuances of sound, and so must actors and readers. To understand his verse, it is of prime importance to read it aloud, observing the usual rules for the speaking of English sentences. A poetic line is not often a sentence: do not confuse the two! A passage reveals its full meaning only when we read it sentence by sentence, carefully observing punctuation.

- If there is no punctuation at the end of a line, make only the slightest of pauses before continuing. Such a line is called **enjambed**, a French term meaning "a striding over." **Enjambment** continues the sense and the grammatical construction of one line into the next line, with neither punctuation nor pause.

- In some lines of poetry, both the sense and the grammatical construction is complete at the end of the line. Such a line is called **end-stopped**, and has a mark of punctuation. When reading, remember that a comma demands a shorter pause than a semicolon or a period.

Scansion involves the division of lines into **feet** in order to determine the **meter**. It is important to scan a passage, exaggerating the **rhythm** to discover the underlying pattern of **stresses,** or **accents**. Note any variations of the norm, which are often crucial clues to meaning. The pattern of **unaccented** and **accented** syllables is usually marked with "x" above an **unaccented** syllable and "/" over an **accented** one.

An **iambic pentameter** line would thus be x / x / x / x / x /. A vertical line "|" divides the feet: x / | x / | x / | x / | x /.

One way to sound out this pattern of **unaccented** and **accented** syllables would be to say the following: da-DUM da-DUM da-DUM da-DUM da-DUM.

Meter is rarely perfectly regular, nor is it meant to be, so a first line is not necessarily a perfect example—scan until you find one that *is* perfect. The study of a few lines reveals which syllables are **stressed** in **disyllabic** words, which have two syllables, and how the function of a **monosyllabic,** or one-syllable word, determines whether it is **accented**. Nouns, verbs, and adjectives are nearly always more significant (and thus more worthy of **stress**) than articles and prepositions.

In listening for the pattern, be aware of **rhetorical accent,** emphasis aside from the **metrical** pattern. Certain syllables receive greater emphasis in order to enhance meaning. Through **scansion** and the correct placing of emphasis, we determine the predominant pattern. Keep in mind that perfectly regular **meter** is silly or hypnotic, suitable only for a nursery rhyme. Substitutions that disturb the regular **rhythm** are frequent and useful, not only for subtlety of sound and complex counterpoint, but also for meaning and emphasis.

Exercise F — Macbeth is urging his wife to behave as though they are the perfect hosts, delighting in their guest's company:

Away, and mock the time with fairest show. (1.7.81)

Consider the importance of adjectives, nouns, and verbs—are they **accented** in this line?

Consider the lesser importance of articles, conjunctions, and prepositions—are they **unaccented**? What is the pattern? How many **feet** are in the line?

Exercise G — Banquo speaks the next lines, seeing the witches for the first time midway through his first line:

How far is't called to Forres?—What are these,
So withered, and so wild in their attire,
That look not like th'inhabitants o'th' earth
And yet are on't? (1.3.37–40)

There are five elisions in these lines. Remember as you read aloud that they compress syllables. Which words are humble little prepositions, articles, and conjunctions that are not likely to be **accented**? Consider the normal pronunciation of the **disyllabic** and **multisyllabic** words, marking the **accented** syllables. What **metrical** pattern should you expect if these are lines from a Shakespeare play? How regular is the pattern in this case?

Exercise H — A very different sound is produced by the witches. The play opens with their words:

> When shall we three meet again?
> In thunder, lightning, or in rain?
> When the hurly-burly's done,
> When the battle's lost and won. (1.1.1–4)

These lines look and sound shorter than the usual **blank verse** lines. To discover the **meter**, mark the **accented** syllables in all the **disyllabic** and **multisyllabic** words. Which other words, especially nouns, verbs, and adjectives, seem to deserve emphasis? Which words do not call attention to themselves? The usual suspects are prepositions, articles, and conjunctions. What **metrical** pattern is formed? Count the syllables and the number of **accents** to discover how many **feet** each line contains. Consult **line length** in the Glossary to find the term for these lines.

Metrical Substitution

Metrical substitution, variations on the basic **metrical** pattern, is essential if the audience is not to be lulled to sleep by a perfectly regular **iambic rhythm**. The most usual **metrical** variations provide emphasis, a pause, or a change in the **pacing**, the speed with which a line is spoken. However, none of these variations is a **metrical foot** which can be easily sustained in English.

A **trochee** (/ x) substituted for an **iamb** (x /), especially at the start of a line, calls attention to that line's first word. The elegant term for this is "initial **trochaic** substitution."

A **spondee** (/ /) substituted for an **iamb** (x /) accents two syllables in a row, also for emphasis.

A **pyrrhic** (x x) substituted for an **iamb** (x /) tends to emphasize the **accent** in the following **foot**.

A **rest**, the absence of a syllable that would make the **foot** regular, breaks the **rhythm** we expect and/or creates a pause, and we look for a reason. A short line, with three feet, for example, produces a long pause.

An **eleventh syllable** at the end of an **iambic pentameter** line, usually **unaccented**, can pick up the **pace**, moving us quickly to the next line or, if the line is **end-stopped**, can provide a greater pause than the punctuation alone.

A **caesura**, a pause or break in the line, variously placed and signaled by punctuation, can modify the regularity of the **meter** in various ways—and is a guide to meaning, **subtext**, and emphasis.

Example

Words to the heat of deeds too cold breath gives. (2.1.61)

Scanned, the line sounds like this:

WORDS to / the HEAT / of DEEDS / TOO COLD / BREATH GIVES.

The meaning is that thought is impaired by words. Thus, *Words*, which is the most important word in this line, is right up front. This order produces an initial **trochaic** substitution. The last two **feet** in the line are both **spondees**, producing pounding emphasis.

Example

Hear it not, Duncan; for it is a knell
That summons thee to heaven or to hell. (2.1.63–64)

Scanned, the lines sound like this:

HEAR it / NOT, DUN / can; for / it is / a KNELL
that SUM / mons THEE / to HEAV / en or / to HELL.

Again, an initial **trochaic** substitution emphasizes the importance of Duncan's not hearing the bell, as does the **spondee** in the second **foot**. The two **pyrrhic feet** cannot be rushed because the two **caesuras** slow down the line, making its meaning more ominous. The **pyrrhic foot** in the last line invites an actor to pause before the **rhyming** word that concludes the scene and prompts his exit: HELL.

Exercise I — Duncan gives the traitor's title to Macbeth, saying:

What he hath lost, noble Macbeth hath won. (1.2.67)

Scan the line, and then label the two substitutions, explaining the effect of each.

Exercise J — Macbeth expresses the need for hypocrisy so their guest, King Duncan, will not suspect foul play:

False face must hide what the false heart doth know. (1.7.82)

Scan the line, and then label the substitutions, explaining the effect of each.

Exercise K — Macbeth is awed by his wife's "mettle" (courage and fortitude):

> **Bring forth men-children only,**
> **For thy undaunted mettle should compose**
> **Nothing but males. (1.7.72–74)**

Scan the lines, taking into account that the first line is shared with the last of Lady Macbeth's words, which are two **iambic feet**. Then label the four substitutions, one used twice, explaining the effect of each.

IV. *Sound Devices*

The witches' words are markedly different from those of the other characters in the play. When Macbeth first approaches them, they display every **sound device** known to poetry, including, of course, **meter** and **rhyme**:

> **The weird sisters hand in hand,**
> **Posters of the sea and land,**
> **Thus do go about, about,**
> **Thrice to thine, and thrice to mine,**
> **And thrice again to make up nine.**
> **Peace! The charm's wound up. (1.3.30–35)**

Example The witches are weaving a magic spell with their ritual words and movements. As they move in a circle, they chant the first five lines, which are full of **rhyme** and **repetition**. They stop circling when they have finished reciting the charm.

The **end rhyme**, rhyme used at the end of each of these short lines, calls attention to itself. An example of **internal rhyme**, sound correspondences that occur in the middle of a line, can be seen within line 4, and is also effective. Frequent **repetition** of words (*hand, about, thrice*) also contributes to the mesmerizing sounds of the charm.

Other effective forms of **repetition** include:

- **Alliteration,** repetition of an initial consonant
- **Assonance,** similar vowel sounds within words, such as the "o" in *posters* and *go*, as well as many sounds in repeated words
- **Consonance**, echoing consonant sounds, as in *sisters* and *posters*. All of these **sound devices** contribute to the **mood** and **atmosphere** of the scene, as does the strong **meter**.

The **meter** works well to enhance the movement. Most lines have four **accents**. The second line, with only three **accents**, hurries along, evoking the witches' swiftness. The **iambic** pattern is broken in lines 2, which begins with a **trochee**. The last line also breaks the pattern, starting with a strong **accent**, "Peace". This forces us to pause and break the **rhythm**, by punching out three **accented** words in a row: "charm's wound up." This last line lets us know that the charm is complete.

The **repetitions** of sounds and movements are hypnotic, even dizzying, as though the witches are dancing their way into a trance in order to tap into their otherworldly power. The audience is drawn into this strange and frightening **mood**, and feels both the power and the dark foreboding evoked by the charm.

V. *Soliloquy*

Many elements work together to reveal Shakespeare's characters in all their complexity. Language is at least as powerful as action. Elizabethans didn't go to *see* a play, but rather to *hear* it. The heightened language of a **soliloquy** makes this set speech much more difficult to follow than a **dialogue**, which often has more conversational language. **Soliloquies** sound unreal to the modern audience. The great ones are often treated either with parody, boredom, or excessive reverence: "To be or not to be" or "But soft, what light through yonder window breaks?"

A **soliloquy** is a response to the immediate situation. For the character who speaks it, it is an attempt to find some resolution, even if this is the speaker's recognition that there is no resolution. For the audience, it is an opportunity to listen and share the character's thoughts and feelings.

A **soliloquy** has more than one function, and keeping the possibilities in mind will help you follow the thought process:

- the character speaking is defined, his reality is strengthened, his secrets are revealed, and he reviews his motives;
- the moral significance of an action already witnessed is revealed, strengthening our understanding;
- the character shares an emotion with the audience, creating either empathy or antagonism;
- in emphasizing what has just happened and anticipating what is to follow, it raises tension for the audience.

VI. *Syntax*

Syntax, a component of grammar, concerns the ordering, grouping, and placement of words in a sentence—the relation of words within the larger unit. The order of words within a sentence is often straightforward in modern English. The core elements are usually grouped together in this order: subject, verb, direct object. All subordinate elements cluster before or after. But Shakespeare's **syntax** is far more complex. In his plays, **inversion of word order** is common. The task of the reader or the actor is first to unscramble difficult **syntax** so that the sentence makes sense, and then consider what is achieved by the **syntactical** ploys.

Disturbances of ordinary **syntax** may involve any of the following:

- separation of related parts: parts of the predicate, adjective and noun, subject and verb, verb and object, etc;
- **inversion**, placing verb before subject, object before subject and verb; and
- phrases, subordinate clauses, etc. separating parts of the main clause.

Shakespeare conveys noteworthy content when he orders words in an unusual way. The king asks, "Dismayed not this our captains, Macbeth and Banquo?" (1.2.34). He is emphasizing the dismay by changing the usual word order, starting with a verb. He later says to the wounded soldier who is reporting to him about the battle, "So well thy words become thee as thy wounds" (1.2.43). The compliment is enhanced by the formal effect of the unusual word order. Shakespeare's **syntax** produces a variety of effects:

- to make the **meter** regular or to end the line with a **rhyme**;
- to raise the level of **diction**, the choice of individual words and patterns of words;

- to produce **parallelism**, presenting similar ideas in a similar manner;
- to emphasize certain words;
- to repeat certain sounds;
- to delay the most important element until last, creating a **periodic sentence**, which withholds either the main clause or the predicate and direct object.

Example   The grandeur of the gift is increased because it is emphasized by being mentioned at the start of the sentence:

> This diamond he greets your wife withal ... (2.1.14)

Ordinary **syntax** would read: "He greets your wife with this diamond."

Example   The **parallelism** of this sentence, as well as the **caesura**, increases the impact of the comparison of *lost* to *won* and emphasizes both words:

> What he hath lost, noble Macbeth hath won. (1.2.67)

Ordinary **syntax** would read: "Noble Macbeth hath won what he hath lost."

Example   After the witches' prophecy to Macbeth, Banquo is eager to know his own future:

> To me you speak not ... (1.3.55)

The emphasis is on the direct object, which is where Banquo wants it to be.

Example   Here are Macbeth's first words in the play:

> "So fair and foul a day I have not seen." (1.3.36)

The key words "fair" and "foul" are emphasized by the **alliteration** of the "*f*" sound that begins each adjective, and by their placement: the entire direct object, "So fair and foul a day," comes before the subject and predicate.

Exercise L — How many of the six effects of syntax listed on page 15 are produced by these nine words?

So well thy words become thee as thy wounds. (1.2.43)

Exercise M — The **periodic sentence** is a common delaying tactic. While a **loose sentence** begins with a subject-verb pair and then provides details, a **periodic sentence** withholds either the main clause, or the predicate and direct object. You will see an example of a **periodic sentence** in the excerpt below.

Here Macbeth is giving his hired assassins their instructions:

Fleance, his son, that keeps him company—
Whose absence is no less material to me
Than is his father's—must embrace the fate
Of that dark hour. (3.1.136–139)

Explain what would be lost if the sentence read: "Fleance must embrace the fate of that dark hour. He is Banquo's son, and he's with his father. His death is as important to me as his father's is."

Exercise N — The bloody soldier uses a **periodic sentence** to tell the king the story of the battle. The rebel enemy is merciless and his followers outnumber those who fight for the king:

15   But all's too weak,
For brave Macbeth—well he deserves that name!—
Disdaining fortune, with his brandished steel
Which smoked with bloody execution,
Like valour's minion
20   Carved out his passage till he faced the slave,
Which ne'er shook hands nor bade farewell to him
Till he unseamed him from the nave to th' chops,
And fixed his head upon our battlements. (1.2.15–23)

Duncan is told that Macbeth committed four actions and omitted to do two others. Mark the six verbs. Then note how many words come between the subject and these predicates. What is the effect of the delay and of the order in which the actions are reported? What purpose does this narrative serve this early in the play, before we have even seen Macbeth?

VII. *Shakespeare in Performance*

The importance of seeing Shakespeare in performance cannot be overstated. Shakespeare did not write his plays to be studied and pored over in classrooms, but to come alive before our eyes on the stage. Fortunately, there is no shortage of opportunities to see Shakespeare performed. Theater companies all over the world—professional, community, and educational—continually produce the bard's plays. Those who cannot see a live production can and should enjoy a wide variety of Shakespearean film and television adaptations.

The classroom study of a Shakespearean play is enriched by focusing on the play as performance, not just as a story in a book. Though **stage directions** are minimal, and sometimes seemingly nonexistent, a close reading of Shakespeare's lines does yield staging **cues** and other clues. Complex sentence structure, as well as language that challenges the silent reader, is easier to understand when the lines are delivered aloud with proper attention to punctuation. The only way to understand all the aspects of Shakespearean language and drama is to read the lines aloud—in the classroom, certainly, but even while reading the plays at home. Readers who can't read aloud (in a library, for example) should "hear" the voices aloud in their heads.

An even better way to visualize what is happening in a Shakespearean play is to get up and move—to act—**in character**, the way the character would behave, while reading the lines. Although it is helpful to study the lines ahead of time, just as any actor would, reading the lines while moving around often clarifies the language, and adds another level of focus to the study.

MACBETH

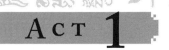

Lesson 1
Paraphrase, Analysis of Ambiguity, Motif

As the play begins, the witches proclaim, **"Fair is foul, and foul is fair"** **(1.1.10).** This statement suggests several meanings, each of which is crucial to our understanding of the witches and Macbeth. Paraphrasing the line, putting the language into your own words, helps the reader to construct meaning and make predictions about the action to follow. Use the guidelines below in order to accurately paraphrase a text:

- Work with one sentence at a time. A line of **blank verse** is not necessarily a sentence. Many lines are **enjambed**. Always paraphrase sentence by sentence, not line by line.

- Use notes provided in your text of the play to find the modern equivalent of unfamiliar or multiple-meaning words.

- Change unusual **syntax** to a word order more common to modern English.

- Consider the **connotations** and how these implied feelings behind individual words create the **tone** of the passage, which indicates the attitude of the speaker. Do not distort the original text by using slang; instead, tune your ear to the author's use of language.

- Take into account both the **figurative** and the **literal** use of language. After unpacking a **metaphor**, a comparison of two unlike things, change the **figurative language** to a **literal**, or matter of fact, interpretation.

- Consider the possibilities of double meanings. The use of the **pun**, a play on two words with similar spelling but different meanings, is quite common in Shakespeare, and may be either comic or serious. If you find a **pun**, include both meanings in your paraphrase, and take a bow.

Example   Arriving at a paraphrase of **"Fair is foul, and foul is fair"** **(1.1.10)**.

Baseball players and fans will have no problem with the two key words. The umpire must make a call if a ball lands near a base line: is the hit a fair or a foul ball? The word *fair* also has an ethical overtone that connotes good or right action, while "foul play" might indicate an action that is morally wrong. A paraphrase might read, "What seems to be good may in fact be evil," or "That which is good may also be evil." Remember that double meanings are always possible.

You could also read this line as "It is not easy to tell the difference between good and evil; in fact, it is easy to confuse the two. Things are not always what they seem." The witches' words are a kind of riddle, which is more than just wordplay; this seemingly simple statement deliberately hides a lie within a truth. This is more than **ambiguity**, in which different meanings are implied—it is **equivocation**, through which the agents of evil purposely mislead Macbeth. The truth of their words will remain hidden until Macbeth finally realizes that appearances can conceal reality. This crucial difference between the apparent and the true is one of the play's major **motifs**, or repeated themes. The **repetition** of this theme greatly enriches the meaning of the play.

Example   When Macbeth first appears in the play two scenes later, his first words are, **"So foul and fair a day I have not seen"** (1.3.36). We are meant to remember the witches' **equivocal** words. The paraphrase might read, "Today has been full of bad weather but glorious victory," which is a **literal** interpretation. But although Macbeth does not hear the witches' pronouncement, we have heard it, and Shakespeare expects that we will connect his words with those of the witches. Is Macbeth already confused about what is real, and what merely seems to be real?

Example   A few lines later, Banquo asks Macbeth about the witches' flattering greeting:

> Good sir, why do you start and seem to fear
> Things that do sound so fair? (1.3.49–50)

A paraphrase might read, "Macbeth, why are you startled and frightened by this good news about your future greatness?" Banquo is pointing out that Macbeth seems afraid of "fair" prophecies as though they were "foul." The **motif** of the discrepancy between appearance and reality is thus continued in this scene.

Lesson 2
Paraphrase, Analysis of Imagery

A **motif** of blood is created by the **repetition** of the image or description of blood in Duncan's first words:

> **What bloody man is that? (1.2.1)**

Duncan is speaking of a wounded soldier, who recounts how Macbeth's sword **"smoked with bloody execution" (1.2.18)** as he performed valorous feats of battle. The gory tale continues as the soldier describes how Macbeth **"Carved out his passage" (1.2.20)** and **"unseamed him from the nave to th' chops, / And fixed his head upon our battlements" (1.2.22–23)**.

Exercise A — Paraphrase each of these four excerpts. As you restate the phrases and lines, use words that capture the meaning of the original text. What is the **literal** meaning of each excerpt?

Exercise B — In these four phrases, *blood* and associated words conjure up **imagery**, description that creates an overall impression and sets a **mood**. List words including nouns, verbs, and modifiers that evoke images. Then comment on the effect of the **repetition** as you respond to the text. Note which of the senses is evoked in each image.

Exercise C — The blood **motif** is also expressed through a **figurative** device, **metonymy**, in which closely related abstract words, here referring to violence, death, and family membership, suggest the image of blood. Make note of examples of this **motif** as it continues throughout 1. 2 and informs the play as a whole. Record any related examples of **metonymy** as you explore the **motif**.

Lesson 3
Analysis of Diction, Antithesis, Characterization

When he sees the witches, Banquo uses several **antitheses**, pairs of opposites, in describing them:

>   —What are these,
> So withered, and so wild in their attire,
> That look not like th'inhabitants o'th'earth
> 40 And yet are on't? —Live you, or are you aught
> That man may question? You seem to understand me
> By each at once her choppy finger laying
> Upon her skinny lips. You should be women,
> And yet your beards forbid me to interpret
> 45 That you are so. (1.3.37–45)

Exercise A — Group the striking adjectives and nouns that Banquo uses. Can you detect a pattern? Are the **connotations** of his **diction** negative or positive?

Exercise B — List the two **antitheses** in the passage, paraphrasing each set of contrasting words and phrases.

Exercise C — How do Banquo's words add to the witches' **characterization**? How does he react to these supernatural beings, and what do his feelings tell us about them?

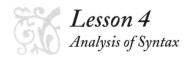

Lesson 4
Analysis of Syntax

The witches greet Macbeth first:

    1ST WITCH   All hail, Macbeth! Hail to thee, Thane of Glamis.

    2ND WITCH   All hail, Macbeth! Hail to thee, Thane of Cawdor.

    3RD WITCH   All hail, Macbeth, that shalt be king hereafter! (1.3.46–48)

Exercise A — Drawing on what you have learned from the earlier scenes, explain why the three titles are presented in this order. Remember that the witches' specialty is making the foul seem fair.

Exercise B — This greeting uses more than mere **repetition**. It also employs the **syntactical** device of **parallelism** to suggest a relationship between ideas. What might the witches intend by greeting Macbeth in this puzzling manner?

Exercise C — Describe the witches' **tone** as it is created by the **repetition** and **parallelism** in this greeting, as well as by its **diction**. Hints: Check the dictionary definition for the word *hail*. Keep in mind that the pronoun *thee* is formal and was suitable for addressing a social superior in Shakespeare's hierarchical England.

Lesson 5
Analysis of Tone, Diction, Syntax

The witches' greeting to Banquo is not as clear as their address to Macbeth, and is full of puzzling **antitheses**:

    1ST WITCH   Lesser than Macbeth, and greater.

    2ND WITCH   Not so happy, yet much happier.

    3RD WITCH   Thou shalt get kings, though thou be none. (1.3.63–65)

Exercise A — List the three sets of words that are **antithetical** (Hint: Two pairs are adjectives, and one is a pair of verbs.) Then paraphrase the greeting, making clear what we learn from this prophecy about Banquo's future as compared to Macbeth's.

Exercise B — Discuss the effect of the **parallelism** in this passage. What does it intensify in the greeting? Why is it important that this prophecy be memorable?

Exercise C — Why do the witches' words to Banquo create **ambiguity**? Is their greeting to Macbeth **ambiguous** in any way? Why or why not?

On Your Feet I
Lessons 3–5

You will be working in small groups—five per group is ideal. **Cast** the section of 1.3 covered in Lessons 3-5 (1.3.37–76) and prepare to enact the scene *after* discussing the lessons. Read the scene aloud once at your desks, then put your books down and stand up. Remembering as much of the encounters as you can, **improvise** the scene with your own words, performing the scene without any previous preparation.

Before returning to Shakespeare's original language, discuss the following questions, using the text for reference:

1. What is Banquo's first reaction when he sees the witches? What is he thinking? How would you describe his emotional state? Which words in lines 37–45 support your viewpoint?

2. Which words will you emphasize in reading this passage aloud? Why? Practice reading aloud with this emphasis in your group.

3. What do you think Macbeth is thinking and feeling—and how will he react physically—as he hears each of the witches' prophecies? Consider what his body language and facial expression will convey as he hears each new prophecy. Practice lines 68–76 in your group, using appropriate body language and facial expressions to convey Macbeth's response to these prophecies.

4. What will each witch emphasize in reciting the next prophecies to Banquo? What are the essential words in lines 63–65? Practice each new prophecy in your group, emphasizing these essential words. Take turns so that each group member works with the text.

5. What makes the witches' prophecies riddles? How do you think Banquo will react to each new riddle?

Review together any words or phrases that are still unclear to you. Next, decide where the witches will be positioned in the classroom, and where Banquo and Macbeth will enter and come upon them. Now you are ready to enact the scene. One group will perform for the class, or a new group will be formed with one student from each original group performing. (If time permits, each group will perform.)

Lesson 6
Figurative Language

The chief figure in Shakespeare's richest passages is **metaphor**, from a Greek word meaning "to transfer." It is useful to speak of the subject of the comparison as the **tenor**, and the image by which the idea is conveyed as the **vehicle**. Their similarities may be called the **grounds**. The easiest figures are **similes** because both the **tenor** and **vehicle** are named, whereas in the various kinds of **metaphor**, one or even both may be unnamed. If these terms get in your way, rather than helping you understand a **metaphor**, just be sure you can identify what's being talked about, what it's being compared to, and how the two things are alike.

The two essential questions to ask in order to unpack a **metaphor** are:

- What two unlike things are being compared?
- What do they have in common?

Metaphors give us a fresh understanding of an ordinary thing or information about an unknown thing through the often surprising, unsuspected similarities the poet has perceived. Common types of **metaphor** include **metonymy** (which you worked with in Lesson 2), **personification**, and **simile**.

Example   When the witches first speak to Macbeth, they hail him as "Thane of Glamis," a noble title that he already has, but also as "Thane of Cawdor," a title held by a nobleman whom Macbeth knows well. Macbeth's response to the witches' greeting doesn't make **literal** or plain sense. The second statement does not seem to follow from the first, and nobody is changing clothes, so we must consider that it is **figurative**. When we can name the true subject, or **tenor**, we will be able to use the qualities of the **vehicle** to discover what is being said about the **tenor**.

> **The Thane of Cawdor lives. Why do you dress me**
> **In borrowed robes?** (1.3.106–107)

Here is an unpacking of Macbeth's **metaphorical** words:

The **tenor** is unstated: Macbeth does not yet know that Cawdor was found to be a traitor and was executed, so he is asking, "Why do you give me a title that belongs to someone else?"

The **vehicle** is stated: "borrowed robes"

The **grounds**, what the two have in common, are the key to the meaning of the **metaphor**. The reader must become part of the creative process in determining which qualities of the **vehicle** can be transferred to the **tenor**. We know that borrowed clothing doesn't fit very well and is not very comfortable. We also know that the borrower must take good care of the clothing so it can be returned unharmed. These qualities can all be carried over to the **tenor**, producing the sense of discomfort and responsibility Macbeth feels in being called by a title that belongs to another.

Example   Banquo's explanation of Macbeth's strange words and behavior is a **simile**, which names both **tenor** and **vehicle**, and uses "like" or "as" to announce a **figurative** comparison. In this case, Banquo not only explains what two unlike things are being compared, he also explains the **grounds**.

> New honours come upon him,
> Like our strange garments, cleave not to their mould
> But with the aid of use. (1.3.143–145)

He speaks not of borrowed robes, but of new garments, to explain Macbeth's strange behavior: his new title will feel rather stiff and ill-fitting until it he has worn it for a while. The clothing **vehicle** becomes a **motif** as the play continues.

Example   **Personification**, a kind of **metaphor** in which nonhuman things are endowed with human characteristics, is used here by Macbeth as he thinks aloud:

> If chance will have me king, why, chance may crown me
> Without my stir. (1.3.142–143)

Here, the idea of "chance" is given the qualities and abilities of a person. The **tenor** is a person powerful enough to crown Macbeth, the **vehicle** is chance, or fate, and the **grounds** are that both chance and a kingmaker have the power and ability to fulfill Macbeth's ambitious desire.

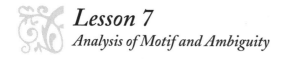

Lesson 7
Analysis of Motif and Ambiguity

Banquo provides a definition of **equivocation** when he warns Macbeth not to trust the witches so completely:

> And oftentimes to win us to our harm
> The instruments of darkness tell us truths,
> Win us with honest trifles to betray's
> In deepest consequence. (1.3.121–124)

Exercise A — Paraphrase the passage. Who are "the instruments of darkness"? What are their motives?

Exercise B — What does Banquo mean by "truths"? How much of the witches' prophecies seems straightforward or true? Which elements seem **ambiguous** or misleading? What **motif** does this passage echo?

Exercise C — Banquo's warning to Macbeth is that, like "fair is foul," the witches' words are **equivocal**. Based on your understanding of his words, and on the two parts of the word ("equi" and "vocal"), define this term for yourself, referring both to the glossary and to an etymological dictionary. How does the witches' **equivocation** create a dilemma for Macbeth?

Lesson 8
Paraphrase Metaphor, Diction

After Duncan has given Macbeth the title "Thane of Cawdor," he names his own eldest son heir to the throne. In an **aside**, which by convention only the audience can hear, Macbeth instantly responds:

> The Prince of Cumberland—that is a step
> On which I must fall down or else o'erleap,
> For in my way it lies. (1.4.48–50)

Exercise A — Paraphrase the passage. What is the obstacle that lies in Macbeth's way?

Exercise B — Identify the **tenor** and **vehicle** of the **metaphor**.

Exercise C — Explain the **grounds** of the **metaphor**. What makes the **vehicle** a successful one? Analyze the possible **connotations** of his words. What are Macbeth's options at this point? Considering the **connotation** of "fall down," which choice does he prefer?

 ## Lesson 9
Paraphrase, Antithesis, Diction

Macbeth's next words introduce two new **motifs**:

> Stars, hide your fires,
> Let not light see my black and deep desires;
> The eye wink at the hand; yet let that be
> Which the eye fears, when it is done, to see. (1.4.50–53)

Exercise A — Paraphrase the passage. List the adjectives and verbs in these lines, and then consider the **connotations** of the **diction**. What **conflicts** or problems are revealed by the word choice?

Exercise B — What **motifs** appear in these lines? What do they add to the overall **atmosphere**? (Hint: Both are **antithetical**: one is a pair of images with opposite **connotations**; the other concerns the difference between appearance and reality.)

Exercise C — What does the word *wink* contribute to Macbeth's **characterization**, especially his moral sense? Based on your close reading of these lines, and considering the use of **antithesis**, explain Macbeth's character as a divided self.

Lesson 10
Analysis of Soliloquy, Metaphor, Diction, Characterization

In her first appearance in the play, Lady Macbeth has just read her husband's letter, and her immediate response to his news is this **soliloquy** from **downstage**. She **characterizes** Macbeth, using **antithesis**, and decides on a plan.

> Glamis thou art, and Cawdor, and shalt be
> What thou art promised. Yet do I fear thy nature.
> 15 It is too full o'th' milk of human kindness
> To catch the nearest way. Thou wouldst be great,
> Art not without ambition, but without
> The illness should attend it. What thou wouldst highly,
> That wouldst thou holily; wouldst not play false,
> 20 And yet wouldst wrongly win. Thou'dst have, great Glamis,
> That which cries 'Thus thou must do' if thou have it,
> And that which rather thou dost fear to do
> Than wishest should be undone. Hie thee hither,
> That I may pour my spirits in thine ear
> 25 And chastise with the valour of my tongue
> All that impedes thee from the golden round
> Which fate and metaphysical aid doth seem
> To have thee crowned withal. (1.5.13–28)

Exercise A — Paraphrase the first sentence, which summarizes the news in the letter. Then unpack the **metaphor** "milk of human kindness." Why is "milk" an appropriate **vehicle**?

Exercise B — Paraphrase the next three sentences (1.16–23). Identify the four sets of **antitheses**, and explain which of Macbeth's character traits is suggested by each. Then explain what Lady Macbeth's plan tells us about her own character.

Exercise C — What is added to Lady Macbeth's **characterization** when you consider her **diction** throughout the passage?

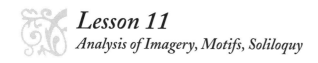

Lesson 11
Analysis of Imagery, Motifs, Soliloquy

Lady Macbeth, awaiting the coming of the king and the opportunity to assassinate him, invokes both evil spirits and night in this rich passage.

> The raven himself is hoarse
> That croaks the fatal entrance of Duncan
> Under my battlements. Come, you spirits
> That tend on mortal thoughts, unsex me here,
> 40 And fill me from the crown to the toe top-full
> Of direst cruelty. Make thick my blood,
> Stop up th'access and passage to remorse,
> That no compunctious visitings of nature
> Shake my fell purpose, nor keep peace between
> 45 Th'effect and it. Come to my woman's breasts,
> And take my milk for gall, you murd'ring ministers,
> Wherever in your sightless substances
> You wait on nature's mischief. Come, thick night,
> And pall thee in the dunnest smoke of hell,
> 50 That my keen knife see not the wound it makes,
> Nor heaven peep through the blanket of the dark
> To cry "Hold, hold! (1.5.36–52)

Exercise A — List the images evoking any of the five senses: touch, taste, sound, smell, and sight. Circle the most vivid **imagery** in each list. Which contribute to **motifs** that have already been established?

Exercise B — Analyze the **diction** in this passage after making three lists of significant nouns, verbs, and modifiers. Describe the **atmosphere** created by these word choices. Then find three sets of **antitheses** and comment on the effect of the contrasts.

Exercise C — Consult the Introduction to remind yourself of the purposes of a **soliloquy**. Which is Shakespeare's central purpose in this speech? Then analyze how this **soliloquy** supplements what we already know about Lady Macbeth. Identify each character trait, and then consider the contribution of **imagery**, **diction**, and **motifs** to the establishment of that trait.

On Your Feet II
Lessons 10 and 11

Working on your own or with a partner, prepare to read one of Lady Macbeth's two **soliloquies** (1.5.13–28 or 1.5.36–52) aloud to the class or to a group within the class. If you are working with a partner, alternate the roles of Lady Macbeth and the messenger, and include the lines between the two **soliloquies** (1.5.29–35) to create a unified presentation.

Consider the following questions before you prepare your **soliloquies**:

1. From what you've read up to this point, what kind of marriage do you think Macbeth and Lady Macbeth have? How might your understanding of their relationship as husband and wife affect the way you will enact the scenes?

2. What does Lady Macbeth's reaction to the letter suggest about her feelings as she waits for Macbeth to return—even before she reads the letter? What might you do to convey that intensity, both vocally and physically? If you are working with a partner, demonstrate how you will convey Lady Macbeth's intensity.

3. Based on your reading of the letter and the **soliloquy**, determine what Lady Macbeth *wants*. What are the key words in the passage that you will emphasize to show her desires and intentions?

4. How is Lady Macbeth's second **soliloquy** in Lesson 11 similar to Macbeth's **aside**, 1.4.48–53, that you studied in Lesson 9? What words or phrases convey this similarity, and how will you play up this language to make the scene work?

5. Whom is Lady Macbeth addressing? What bodily position or gestures will best convey Lady Macbeth's pleas: Might she stand? Sit? Kneel? Lie prostrate? Justify your choice, and demonstrate this body language and posture if you are working with a partner.

6. What words and phrases are gender-related, reminding us— and Lady Macbeth herself—that she is a woman? How might you call attention to these as you read the **soliloquy** aloud?

Review the **soliloquies** to discuss any words or phrases that you find difficult. Practice the scene and prepare to read aloud before the class or a portion of the class, using the gestures and vocal emphasis you have planned.

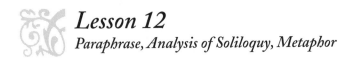

Lesson 12
Paraphrase, Analysis of Soliloquy, Metaphor

Macbeth's complex **soliloquy** is easier to follow if it is divided into five parts, as is indicated here with ☸.

> If it were done when 'tis done, then 'twere well
> It were done quickly. If th'assassination
> Could trammel up the consequence, and catch
> With his surcease success: that but this blow
> 5 Might be the be-all and end-all, here,
> But here upon this bank and shoal of time,
> We'd jump the life to come. But in these cases
> We still have judgement here, that we but teach
> Bloody instructions which, being taught, return
> 10 To plague th'inventor. This even-handed justice
> Commends th'ingredience of our poisoned chalice
> To our own lips. ☸ He's here in double trust:
> First, as I am his kinsman and his subject,
> Strong both against the deed; then, as his host,
> 15 Who should against the murderer shut the door,
> Not bear the knife myself. ☸ Besides, this Duncan
> Hath borne his faculties so meek, hath been
> So clear in his great office, that his virtues
> Will plead like angels, trumpet-tongued against
> 20 The deep damnation of his taking-off, ☸
> And pity, like a naked new-born babe,
> Striding the blast, or heaven's cherubin, horsed
> Upon the sightless couriers of the air,
> Shall blow the horrid deed in every eye
> 25 That tears shall drown the wind. ☸ I have no spur
> To prick the sides of my intent, but only
> Vaulting ambition which o'erleaps itself
> And falls on th'other. (1.7.1–28)

Exercise A — Find Macbeth's practical and ethical objections to the murder scheme and explain them in a paraphrase.

Exercise B — Find Macbeth's religious and visionary objections to the murder scheme and explain them in a paraphrase.

Exercise C — Find and unpack the **metaphor** about a horse and rider, and discuss what it contributes to the list of objections.

 Lesson 13
Analysis of Diction, Prosody, Metaphor, Motifs

After Macbeth has persuaded himself and told his wife that he will not murder the king, she responds to his qualms with impatience, which she expresses through **personification**:

35   Was the hope drunk
         Wherein you dressed yourself? Hath it slept since?
         And wakes it now to look so green and pale
         At what it did so freely? From this time
         Such I account thy love. Art thou afeard
40   To be the same in thine own act and valour
         As thou art in desire? Wouldst thou have that
         Which thou esteem'st the ornament of life,
         And live a coward in thine own esteem,
         Letting 'I dare not' wait upon 'I would',
45   Like the poor cat i'th' adage? (1.7.35–45)

Exercise A — Lady Macbeth goads her husband into action by means of the three questions that begin the passage. Unpack the **metaphor**, and then paraphrase these questions.

Exercise B — Discuss what the passage contributes to several **motifs** established earlier in the play, such as the **antithesis** between light and darkness and the associations that apply to gender.

Exercise C — The **tone** of the passage is created to a great extent by an aspect of its **diction**. Read the passage aloud several times, noting Lady Macbeth's frequent use of **monosyllabic** words. What is the effect of this barrage of one-syllable words? (Checking the **literal** meaning of *barrage* in a dictionary will be helpful.) In contrast, what is the effect of the few **disyllabic** and **polysyllabic** words? Analyze what this **diction** contributes to the **tone**.

Lesson 14
Analysis of Prosody, Syntax, Antithesis, Sound Devices, Tone

In his response, Macbeth reacts to his wife's accusation:

> I dare do all that may become a man;
> Who dares do more is none. (1.7.46–47)

Exercise A — Use a dictionary to discover what Macbeth means by *become*. Then paraphrase the passage.

Exercise B — Comment on the effect of the **parallelism**, **antithesis**, and **sound devices** of the passage.

Exercise C — Consider how Macbeth's **tone** is created by the use of a single **disyllabic** word among many **monosyllables**. Identify the **motif** introduced here.

Lesson 15
Paraphrase, Analysis of Syntax

Lady Macbeth responds with these words:

> When you durst do it, then you were a man;
> And to be more than what you were, you would
> Be so much more the man. (1.7.49–51)

Exercise A — Paraphrase the passage. Compare how Lady Macbeth's definition of manliness differs from her husband's.

Exercise B — What is the effect of the **parallelism** in these lines? Explain the suggestions implied by "be more" and "so much more."

Exercise C — Compare the language and content of this passage to Lady Macbeth's words in Lesson 11.

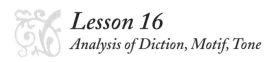

Lesson 16
Analysis of Diction, Motif, Tone

Lady Macbeth continues her verbal assault:

> I have given suck, and know
> How tender 'tis to love the babe that milks me.
> I would, while it was smiling in my face,
> Have plucked my nipple from his boneless gums
> And dashed the brains out, had I so sworn
> As you have done to this. (1.7.54–59)

Exercise A — List and categorize the strong words in this extraordinary statement, as nouns, verbs, and modifiers. Then consider how the speech connects to the manliness **motif** that precedes it.

Exercise B — What does Lady Macbeth's **diction** contribute to the **tone** of the passage?

Exercise C — Compare this passage with those in Lessons 10 and 11. What do they have in common? How does this speech reflect the **motif** about manliness? Can one gender be discussed without the other?

On Your Feet III
Lessons 13–16

Work in pairs as you prepare to enact this **dialogue** between Macbeth and Lady Macbeth. Because Lessons 1–12 have prepared you to read and understand the scene's words and **subtext**—the real intentions beneath the words of the text—your teacher may assign this *On Your Feet* activity before *or* after doing Lessons 13–16. You know what Lady Macbeth wants, and you understand Macbeth's indecision and moral misgivings at this point. Imagine a modern scene in which a wife wants her husband to do something abhorrent and attacks his manhood. Your teacher will ask you to write out, **improvise**, or briefly describe your modern example, using what you already know about Act I of *Macbeth* to inform your choices. Then consider and discuss the following:

1. Review and/or list all the gender references (specific lines referring to manliness or womanliness) which have led up to this scene. How might these earlier references affect the way you enact the scene?

2. Look closely at this scene (1.7.28–82) for more gender references that build on those you have seen earlier in the act. Consider how you will emphasize each of these references when you read. Select two of these references, and practice them aloud with your partner.

3. Think about both characters' body language and physical positioning in the scene. Show your partner where you think each character should stand and move in relationship to one another and to the audience.

4. Where is the tension between the two characters at its greatest in this scene? Mark in your scripts the places where the tension is most heightened. Show your partner how you will create this tension vocally and physically and how you will allow it to build as you enact the scene.

Now look over the scene and review any words or phrases that may be difficult to read aloud. Rehearse the scene, paying special attention to body language, positioning, and vocal tension. Be ready to volunteer to read in class. Two volunteers from different pairs will read the scene for the class.

Lesson 17
Paraphrase, Characterization

On the night of Duncan's murder, Banquo resists sleep. This passage introduces the **motif** of sleep and dreams, which continues throughout the play:

> A heavy summons lies like lead upon me,
> And yet I would not sleep. Merciful powers,
> Restrain in me the cursèd thoughts that nature
> Gives way to in repose. (2.1.6–9)

A moment later, Macbeth enters, and the two men speak of the witches' prophecies. In this **dialogue**, Banquo makes his feelings about the prophecies quite clear. We already know Macbeth's feelings:

> BANQUO   I dreamt last night of the three weird sisters.
> To you they have showed some truth.
> 20   MACBETH   I think not of them;
> Yet, when we can entreat an hour to serve,
> We would spend it in some words upon that business
> If you would grant the time.
> BANQUO   At your kind'st leisure.
> MACBETH   If you shall cleave to my consent when 'tis,
> It shall make honour for you.
> 25   BANQUO   So I lose none
> In seeking to augment it, but still keep
> My bosom franchised and allegiance clear,
> I shall be counselled. (2.1.19-26)

Exercise A — Recalling the witches' prophecy to him, paraphrase Banquo's words in the first passage. What thought does he fear? Why?

Exercise B — Paraphrase the **dialogue** between Banquo and Macbeth.

Exercise C — Explain Banquo's role in this **dialogue** as a **foil**, or
contrast, to Macbeth, highlighting Macbeth's character through
contrast to his own.

Lesson 18
Analysis of Diction, Metaphor, Atmosphere, Ambiguity

Macbeth speaks here in **soliloquy**:

> Is this a dagger which I see before me,
> The handle toward my hand? Come, let me clutch thee.
> 35   I have thee not, and yet I see thee still.
> Art thou not, fatal vision, sensible
> To feeling as to sight? Or art thou but
> A dagger of the mind, a false creation
> Proceeding from the heat-oppressèd brain?
> 40   I see thee yet, in form as palpable
> As this which now I draw.
> Thou marshall'st me the way that I was going,
> And such an instrument I was to use.
> Mine eyes are made the fools o'th' other senses,
> 45   Or else worth all the rest. I see thee still,
> And on thy blade and dudgeon gouts of blood,
> Which was not so before. There's no such thing.
> It is the bloody business which informs
> Thus to mine eyes. Now o'er the one half-world
> 50   Nature seems dead, and wicked dreams abuse
> The curtained sleep. Witchcraft celebrates
> Pale Hecate's offerings, and withered murder,
> Alarumed by his sentinel the wolf,
> Whose howl's his watch, thus with his stealthy pace,
> 55   With Tarquin's ravishing strides, towards his design
> Moves like a ghost. Thou sure and firm-set earth,
> Hear not my steps which way they walk, for fear

Thy very stones prate of my whereabout,
And take the present horror from the time,
60   Which now suits with it. Whiles I threat, he lives.
Words to the heat of deeds too cold breath gives.
[A bell rings]
I go, and it is done. The bell invites me.
Hear it not, Duncan; for it is a knell
That summons thee to heaven or to hell. (2.1.33–64)

Exercise A — Personification adds to the richness of the **imagery** in this passage. Eleven inanimate objects, nonhumans, or abstract ideas are given human characteristics; list them along with their traits.

Exercise B — Describe the **mood** or **atmosphere** created by the **diction**. What three new **motifs** are introduced in this **soliloquy**?

Exercise C — Explain what is **ambiguous** in Macbeth's experience of the dagger, the night, and the bell.

On Your Feet IV
Lesson 18

Working on your own or with a partner, prepare to deliver Macbeth's famous "bloody dagger" **soliloquy** (2.1.33–64) to the class. Use your responses to Lesson 18, Exercise B, to help you determine the kind of **mood** and **atmosphere** you will create vocally in the **soliloquy**. Notice those lines in Macbeth's speech where the **mood** and vocal inflections might subtly change. Answer these questions with your partner and follow the directions below as you prepare the **soliloquy**:

1. How would you feel—and more specifically, how you would react—if you were contemplating murder and a dagger suddenly appeared before you in mid-air? How would you move? Would you go toward the dagger, trying to hold it, or would you move away from it?

2. Which lines indicate Macbeth's uncertainty about whether or not the dagger is real—and how will you act out this uncertainty? Practice these lines with your partner, showing how you will convey Macbeth's disbelief in what he thinks he sees.

3. According to the text, what does Macbeth do as he speaks the lines "I see thee yet, in form as palpable / As this which now I draw"? With your partner, practice how you will reconcile this action with your physical movement as you engage with the dagger of Macbeth's apparition.

4. How does the apparition change for Macbeth in lines 44–47? How do you think Macbeth responds to this change, and how can you show his response with body language and facial expressions? Demonstrate these gestures and expressions to your partner.

5. Why is a change in vocal **tone** appropriate as Macbeth says, "Now o'er the one half world..." in the middle of line 49? How would you describe this change in **tone**, and when does it shift again? Practice emphasizing Macbeth's **tone** shifts with your partner.

6. What does Macbeth decide with certainty during the closing lines of the **soliloquy**? What gestures and bodily stance might you use to convey this decision? Show your partner how you will read these lines to express conviction and determination.

Try to familiarize yourself with the **soliloquy** so that you don't need to rely heavily on your book but can look up once in a while. You might consider committing the **soliloquy** (or possibly a few of its lines) to memory. Several students will perform their **soliloquies** for the class or for a section of the class.

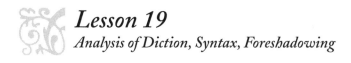

Lesson 19
Analysis of Diction, Syntax, Foreshadowing

Macbeth returns to his wife with bloody hands, reporting the words of the drugged guards and expressing his fear that his act is damning:

> MACBETH   One cried 'God bless us' and 'Amen' the other,
> 25   As they had seen me with these hangman's hands.
> List'ning their fear I could not say 'Amen'
> When they did say 'God bless us.'
> LADY MACBETH   Consider it not so deeply.
> MACBETH   But wherefore could not I pronounce 'Amen'?
> 30   I had most need of blessing, and 'Amen'
> Stuck in my throat. (2.2.24–31)

Macbeth next tells his wife of a disembodied voice depriving him of sleep and seeming to **foreshadow** or predict an unforeseen consequence of the murder. He describes his feelings about sleep in a series of **metaphors**:

> Methought I heard a voice cry 'Sleep no more,
> Macbeth does murder sleep'—the innocent sleep,
> Sleep that knits up the ravelled sleave of care,
> The death of each day's life, sore labour's bath,
> Balm of hurt minds, great nature's second course,
> Chief nourisher in life's feast— (2.2.33–38)

Exercise A — Discuss the roles, in the first passage, of **diction** and **repetition** in dramatizing this first symptom of a change in Macbeth as a result of the murder.

Exercise B — Consult a dictionary to find the meaning of the archaic word *sleave*. Unpack the four **metaphors** in the second passage that use **personification** to explain the vital importance of sleep. Then unpack the remaining two **metaphors**.

Exercise C — What controlling idea unifies the series of **metaphors**? What **motif** and problem does this passage **foreshadow**, or hint at?

Lesson 20
Analysis of Diction, Prosody, Characterization

After the murder, Lady Macbeth enjoins her husband to "Go get some water / And wash this filthy witness from your hand" (2.2.44–45). She then tries to send him back with the daggers to frame the grooms, but must go herself. Macbeth speaks in **soliloquy**:

> What hands are here! Ha, they pluck out mine eyes.
> Will all great Neptune's ocean wash this blood
> Clean from my hand? No, this my hand will rather
> The multitudinous seas incarnadine,
> Making the green one red. (2.2.57–61)

When she returns from the grisly task, Lady Macbeth goads her husband:

> My hands are of your colour, but I shame
> To wear a heart so white. (2.2.62–63)

Exercise A — List the strong nouns, verbs, and modifiers in the first passage. What does his **diction** reveal about Macbeth's emotional state?

Exercise B — Read the first passage aloud several times, observing the pauses signaled by punctuation. Then look at the individual lines. When a line with ten or eleven syllables (the first and third lines) contains ten or more separate words, each a **monosyllable**, is it fast or slow? Compare these with the fourth line, which has eleven syllables, but only four words; count the syllables in the two **polysyllabic** words. Discuss the difference in the **pacing**, or speed, of the spoken line and the effect of the contrast.

Exercise C — Sum up how Lady Macbeth's words in the second passage **characterize** her. In what sense is Macbeth the **foil** to his wife here? Is she also a **foil** to her husband? Why or why not?

On Your Feet V

Lessons 19 and 20

Work in groups of four as you prepare to enact the end of Act 2, Scene 2, from "One cried..." in line 24 to the end of the scene. Choose two students to read the scene while you are all seated at your desks; the other two will listen and react without looking at the text. The listeners will provide the "knocking" sound effects in line 55 and will offer feedback on the scene's clarity to the readers.

Discuss and practice the following as you prepare to enact this scene:

1. How does Macbeth react to the prediction that he will not be able to sleep? Think about how an agitated person who cannot sleep might feel. In your group, discuss how this agitation might be expressed physically and vocally, and show your group members how such a distraught, sleep-deprived person might act and sound. Use some of the text's lines for your demonstration.

2. How is the thought of not being able to sleep intertwined with Macbeth's reaction to having murdered Duncan? Cite lines to support the connection between the murder and Macbeth's fear that he will be unable to sleep.

3. If you hear an unexpected noise when you're already intensely agitated, how do you react? Demonstrate this reaction to your group. Note that Macbeth's startled response to the knocking comes at the time when the tension of the scene is already building rapidly. Practice increasing the vocal tension as you react to the knocking.

4. In his **soliloquy**, Macbeth obsesses over his blood-soaked hands. He uses hyperbole, exaggeration to create an effect, when he says that the entire ocean couldn't wash this blood from him. As you perform these lines, what kinds of gestures might you use to maintain the focus and tension? Take turns demonstrating within your group.

After you've answered these questions and practiced reading and stage movement, you are ready to enact the scene. Take turns, possibly changing partners within your group. Have each pair act out the scene incorporating the vocal emphasis, tension, gestures and physical movement you've planned.

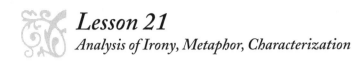

Lesson 21
Analysis of Irony, Metaphor, Characterization

After Duncan's murder has been discovered, Macbeth addresses the horrified and frightened nobility in a speech loaded with both **verbal irony**, in which he says the opposite of what he means, and **dramatic irony**, created by the audience's knowing something that Macbeth doesn't know.

> Had I but died an hour before this chance
> I had lived a blessèd time, for from this instant
> There's nothing serious in mortality.
> All is but toys. Renown and grace is dead.
> The wine of life is drawn, and the mere lees
> Is left this vault to brag of. (2.3.87–92)

Exercise A — Consult a dictionary for the meaning of *grace* and *lees*. How does Macbeth describe the world, in the wake of Duncan's murder? What is he really saying about himself? Now unpack the **metaphors** in the last two sentences.

Exercise B — What do Macbeth's words here add to his **characterization**? How can we account for his calm reasoning, considering his immediate response to the murder?

Exercise C — What is **ironic** in this speech of Macbeth's? Can you detect **verbal** and/or **dramatic irony**? How does Macbeth actually feel as a result of the murder?

Act **3**

Lesson 22
Review of Literary Terms

Having decided to murder Banquo and his son before the banquet, Macbeth ends his invitation to Banquo with these words:

Fail not our feast. (3.1.29)

What is chilling about these four simple words? Find which four of the following literary devices help achieve the effect: **metaphor, diction, alliteration, imagery, ambiguity, parallelism, dramatic irony, monosyllables, syntax, foreshadowing**. Explain what each of the four devices contributes.

Lesson 23
Paraphrase, Analysis of Diction, Characterization

Just before he hires assassins to kill Banquo, Macbeth, in **soliloquy**, considers the witches' prophecy about Banquo's sons inheriting the throne:

> To be thus is nothing
> 50 But to be safely thus. Our fears in Banquo
> Stick deep, and in his royalty of nature
> Reigns that which would be feared. 'Tis much he dares,
> And to that dauntless temper of his mind
> He hath a wisdom that doth guide his valour
> 55 To act in safety. There is none but he
> Whose being I do fear, and under him
> My genius is rebuked as, it is said,
> Mark Antony's was by Caesar. He chid the sisters
> When first they put the name of king upon me,
> 60 And bade them speak to him. Then, prophet-like,
> They hailed him father to a line of kings.

Upon my head they put a fruitless crown,
And put a barren scepter in my grip,
Thence to be wrenched with an unlineal hand,
65 No son of mine succeeding. If't be so,
For Banquo's issue have I filed my mind,
For them the gracious Duncan have I murdered,
Put rancours in the vessel of my peace
Only for them, and mine eternal jewel
70 Given to the common enemy of man
To make them kings, the seeds of Banquo kings.
Rather than so, come fate into the list
And champion me to th'utterance. (3.1.49–73)

Exercise A — Again Shakespeare makes Banquo a **foil** for Macbeth. Paraphrase the sentences in which Banquo's traits are described, then explain how each of Macbeth's is an opposite.

Exercise B — What do we learn about Macbeth's state of mind from his **diction** and **repetitions** in the **soliloquy**?

Exercise C — Paraphrase the last eight lines of the **soliloquy**. Is Macbeth newly aware of the consequences of his crime, or had he always known that these were inevitable? Then paraphrase and comment on Macbeth's beliefs about fate or chance: Does he trust or mistrust the witches and their prophecies?

Lesson 24
Paraphrase, Analysis of Irony, Prosody, Syntax, Antithesis

In the next scene, Lady Macbeth delivers two **couplets** that are rich in meaning and emotion. **Couplets** normally end a scene, but this speech is made early in the 3.2 she speaks in **soliloquy**:

Naught's had, all's spent,
Where our desire is got without content.
'Tis safer to be that which we destroy
Than by destruction dwell in doubtful joy. (3.2.6–9)

A troubled Macbeth soon joins his wife, and she advises him:

Things without all remedy
Should be without regard. What's done is done. (3.2.13–14)

Exercise A — Paraphrase these two sets of two sentences each.

Exercise B — Describe the effect of the **parallelism, antithesis,** and **rhyme** in expressing Lady Macbeth's feelings when she is alone (lines 6 to 9).

Exercise C — How does Lady Macbeth's use of **parallelism** and **repetition** achieve a different effect in lines 13 and 14, when she speaks to her husband? Comment on the **dramatic irony**.

 # *Lesson 25*
Analysis of Metaphor, Motif, and Irony

Macbeth replies with these brooding words:

15   We have scorched the snake, not killed it.
She'll close and be herself, whilst our poor malice
Remains in danger of her former tooth.
But let the frame of things disjoint, both the worlds suffer,
Ere we will eat our meal in fear, and sleep
20   In the affliction of these terrible dreams
That shake us nightly. Better be with the dead,
Whom we to gain our peace have sent to peace,
Than on the torture of the mind to lie
In restless ecstasy. Duncan is in his grave.
25   After life's fitful fever he sleeps well. (3.2.15–25)

Exercise A — Unpack the **metaphor** in the first two sentences. Then paraphrase the remaining three sentences.

Exercise B — The **motif** of sleep and dreaming recurs here. What is its **ironic** effect in this passage?

Lesson 26
Analysis of Sound Devices, Syntax, and Irony

When Lady Macbeth makes the suggestion that Banquo and Fleance are mortals, and thus may be murdered in their turn, Macbeth responds with these words:

> There's comfort yet, they are assailable.
> Then be thou jocund. Ere the bat hath flown
> His cloistered flight, ere to black Hecate's summons
> The shard-borne beetle with his drowsy hums
> Hath rung night's yawning peal, there shall be done
> A deed of dreadful note. (3.2.40–44)

Exercise A — Mark and comment on the effect of the **sound devices** in this passage: **assonance, consonance, alliteration,** and **onomatopoeia,** in which the sound of the word suggests its meaning.

Exercise B — Note and comment on the effect of **diction, allusion** (a reference to a familiar historical or literary figure, event, or object), and **imagery**. What **ironies** can you find? Which details create the dark **atmosphere** of the passage?

Exercise C — The third sentence in this passage is a long one. Analyze its **syntax** and describe the effect of this **periodic sentence** on the **atmosphere** of the passage. Would the main clause be more or less effective if it displayed the usual word order of subject-verb?

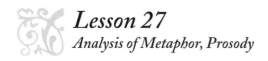

Lesson 27
Analysis of Metaphor, Prosody

While waiting for night to fall so that his hired murderers can ambush Banquo and his son, Macbeth **apostrophizes** night, addressing it as if it could understand him, and describes the scene for us. **Scene-painting** is essential in Shakespeare's theater—remember that performances were in broad daylight, so the actor's words supply vivid **imagery**.

> Come, seeling night,
> Scarf up the tender eye of pitiful day,
> And with thy bloody and invisible hand
> 50 Cancel and tear to pieces that great bond
> Which keeps me pale. Light thickens, and the crow
> Makes wing to th' rooky wood.
> Good things of day begin to droop and drowse,
> Whiles night's black agents to their preys do rouse. (3.2.47–54)

Exercise A — Paraphrase the passage, translating the **figurative** language in the first sentence into its **literal** meaning. (Hint: two things are **personified** in the passage.)

Exercise B — Analyze the effect of the **sound devices** in the passage. How do certain sounds intensify the **tone**? Then analyze the effects of the **diction** and **imagery**.

Exercise C — How does the series of **monosyllables** effect the shifting **tone** of the passage? (Hint: **monosyllables** may be read either slowly or in brisk staccato.)

On Your Feet VI
Lessons 26 and 27

Lessons 26 and 27 focused on two short speeches, Act 3, Scene 2, lines 40–44 and 47–54. Both of these speeches use **sound devices** extensively. In a group of two to six students, read the speeches aloud, emphasizing not only the **sound devices** but the visual **imagery** of night as well. Choose one of the two speeches for memorization.

Discuss and practice the following questions in your group:

1. Look back at Lesson 26, Exercise A, and identify examples of **sound devices** for vocal emphasis. Practice saying words like *hum* (**onomatopoeia**) and phrases like "there shall be done / A deed of dreadful note" (**alliteration**—emphasize the "d" sounds), and exaggerate the **sound devices**. Don't be afraid to go way over the top with your exaggerations. Over-emphasizing these devices as you practice will help you to be aware of them so that you will give them appropriate emphasis in performance.

2. Practice the speech from Lesson 27 with the same degree of exaggerated emphasis. Stress not only the language using **sound devices**, but the phrases with visual **imagery** as well; decide with your group which words need the most emphasis.

3. Note especially Lesson 27 Exercise C, and practice emphasizing each **monosyllable** distinctly. How do the words *droop* and *drowse* affect the **pacing** of this **monosyllabic** line? Practice drawing these words out with exaggerated emphasis in the context of line 53.

Several volunteers will read one of these two speeches expressively for the class, or your teacher may have you read these speeches in the context of the closing lines of 3.2.

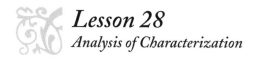

Lesson 28
Analysis of Characterization

The short scene of Banquo's murder and Fleance's escape begins with the first and second murderers questioning a third who has mysteriously joined them. Who is this person and why has he joined the hired killers? Prepare to argue a side in a debate on this issue. One theory is that the third murderer is Macbeth himself, disguising himself for a meeting because he is unable to trust his hired assassins. What evidence do we have that Macbeth is mistrustful? Does he have reason to be? Another theory is that this person is a trusted agent of Macbeth's whose task will be to murder the hired assassins once they have done their job. What evidence do you have that Macbeth has the practical or psychological need to eliminate those who murder Banquo? Plan your side's argument by collecting evidence from earlier in the play, then let the debate begin.

On Your Feet VII
Act 3, Scene 3

The third scene of Act 3 is an exciting scene for classroom performance, especially after your classroom debate about the identity of the third murderer. Your teacher will decide whether you will perform the scene once, as a class, or if you will work on the scene in your small groups. Either way, you need to read through the scene once on your own, thinking about **blocking**, which includes all stage movements, entrances, and exits.

Group directions and scene preparation questions:

1. **Cast** the scene within your group, choosing the actors who will play the various roles.

2. Discuss the mental and emotional state of the two murderers. What are they thinking and feeling as they prepare to kill Banquo? What is their attitude toward an unexpected third murderer? Your answers to these questions will help you to plan their bodily stances and positions.

3. Discuss and practice how the murderers will react physically when they hear the sound of horses (3.3.8).

4. Decide where Banquo and Fleance will enter. Remember that Fleance is carrying a torch; either pantomime the torch or use a makeshift **prop**.

5. Discuss the **tone** of Banquo's words "It will be rain tonight" and the sudden violence of the murderer's words "Let it come down." How will you play these lines for the maximum tension and effect?

6. At what point will Fleance run away, and in which direction? How will the murderers react as Fleance escapes?

Lesson 29
Analysis of Tone, Diction, Motif

During the banquet, Macbeth alone sees the ghost of Banquo, and his terrified reaction causes his wife to draw him aside and caution him:

> LADY MACBETH   Are you a man?
>
> MACBETH   Ay, and a bold one, that dare look on that
> Which might appal the devil.
>
> LADY MACBETH   O proper stuff!
>
> 60   This is the very painting of your fear;
> This is the air-drawn dagger which you said
> Led you to Duncan. O, these flaws and starts,
> Impostors to true fear, would well become
> A woman's story at a winter's fire
>
> 65   Authorized by her grandam. Shame itself,
> Why do you make such faces? When all's done
> You look but on a stool. . . .
>
>   . . .What, quite unmanned in folly?
>   . . . Fie, for shame! (3.4.57–67, 72, 73)

Exercise A — List examples of the **diction** that Lady Macbeth uses to shame her husband. What language does Macbeth use to defend himself against her charges?

Exercise B — Analyze how the **diction** in this **dialogue** creates the **tone** of each speaker.

Exercise C — How is the **motif** of manliness used by husband and wife in this **dialogue**? Is there evidence that their relationship has changed during the course of their bloody career?

Lesson 30
Paraphrase, Analysis of Tone, Syntax

After Lady Macbeth has hurried away the guests, Macbeth mutters ancient superstitions that murderers will be exposed:

> It will have blood, they say. Blood will have blood.
> Stones have been known to move, and trees to speak,
> Augurs and understood relations have
> By maggot-pies and choughs and rooks brought forth
> The secret'st man of blood. (3.4.121–125)

Exercise A — What is Macbeth's primary emotion in this passage? How does **repetition** create his **tone**? Paraphrase the line "blood will have blood."

Exercise B — What is the effect of his references to stones, trees, and birds?

Exercise C — How does this revelation of Macbeth's beliefs connect to his trust in the witches' prophecies?

Lesson 31
Paraphrase, Analysis of Metaphor, Diction

Having resolved to seek out the witches and demand "by the worst means the worst" (line 134), Macbeth describes his situation:

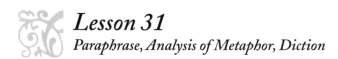

>   I am in blood
> Stepped in so far that, should I wade no more,
> Returning were as tedious as go o'er. (3.4.135–137)

Exercise A — Unpack the **metaphor**. Paraphrase what Macbeth **literally** means.

Exercise B — Consider the effect of the word *tedious*. In modern English, the word means tiresome, boring, or wearying by reason of length, slowness, or dullness. In Shakespeare's era, the word had a different meaning, referring to a slow movement or progression. Analyze Macbeth's statement in light of what *tedious* meant to an Elizabethan audience.

Exercise C — Considering the original **connotation** of *tedious*, what does this passage reveal about Macbeth's feelings at this point?

On Your Feet VIII
Lessons 29–31: Macbeth's Banquet

The banquet scene in Act 3, Scene 4, is one of vivid spectacle when the play is produced. In addition to the speaking characters, the stage is filled with lords and ladies in resplendent finery and several attendants. Banquo's Ghost, unseen by any except Macbeth, inspires the murderous king's lunatic ravings. We recognize just how crazed and bloodthirsty Macbeth has become, and we see the effects of his actions on Scotland. Performing this entire scene as a class, with everyone participating, is the best way to feel in your bones the horror and tension of the scene.

Your teacher will direct you to arrange your classroom desks or tables so that you have a long banquet table with two seats for the monarchs at the front of the room. Lady Macbeth is seated near the head of the table while Macbeth moves cheerfully toward his guests on "Ourself will mingle with society." A seat is left for Macbeth at the head of the table, but it is essential that *only* this one seat is left vacant. Be sure to remove any extra chairs before you begin the scene.

Scene preparation directions and questions:

1. The following roles will be assigned: Macbeth, First Murderer, Second Murderer, Lady Macbeth, Banquo's Ghost, Ross, and Lennox. Everyone else will be a lord or lady, reading the lines marked "Lords" in unison for maximum effect. Those playing the murderers should return to the table to double as lords and ladies.

2. Read through the scene silently, looking for implied stage directions. Although Shakespeare did not provide detailed **stage directions**, actions are often implied in the lines. For example, in the opening line of the scene, Macbeth speaks to his guests, saying, "You know your own degrees; sit down." His guests know their own rank and understand where they should sit at the table. Although there is no specific **stage direction**, you should sit when you hear this line unless you are playing a murderer or the Ghost.

3. If you have individual speaking lines, be sure you review them before performing the scene. This will help you to pick up your cues and avoid leaving an awkward break between lines.

4. If you are a lord or lady, look for the places where you will rise and toast.

5. Look closely at the **stage directions** indicating when Banquo appears. Note what Macbeth has said or is saying at almost the exact moment when the ghost appears. Why is there **irony** and black humor in the ghost's specific appearances?

6. The lords have a line during Macbeth's reaction of amazement and horror as he first sees Banquo's Ghost: "What, my good lord?" (3.4.48) This line should *not* be delivered in unison by all the guests, even though the line is attributed to "lords." Instead, what might the lords and ladies do or say at this point? Consider how a looser interpretation of the **stage directions** actually improves the scene.

7. Keep in mind that, as guests, you are watching your sovereign, the ruler of your country, go mad before your eyes. What might you, as one of Macbeth's subjects, realize about your king? How will you react to Macbeth's ravings—what might you whisper and do?

8. Lady Macbeth sends all the guests away when she says, "At once, good night: / Stand not upon the order of your going, / But go at once." (3.4.117–119) Describe how all the guests, including Ross and Lennox, should leave; as lords and ladies, how will you act as you go?

Return to seats at the back of the classroom and leave the "stage" to Macbeth and Lady Macbeth for the final lines.

On Your Feet IX
Act 3, Scene 5

Scholars agree that Act 3, scene 5 was not written by Shakespeare but by Thomas Middleton, a contemporary of Shakespeare's, for an unsuccessful play called *The Witch*. Nevertheless, the scene is always included in texts of *Macbeth*, and it is usually performed when the play is produced. Your task is to **block** and enact these lines as you would do in an actual production of the play. Your teacher will direct you to prepare the scene as a class or in groups, depending on the size of your class.

Scene preparation questions and directions:

1. Read through Hecate's lines and the spirits' lines once with several students chanting or singing as the spirits. Exaggerate the **meter, rhythm**, and **rhyme** as you read; then compare it to that used by the witches in 1.1 and 1. 3. Consider the regularity of **meter** and **end rhyme** in this passage, compared to the irregularities and frequent lack of **rhyme** in the words of Shakespeare's witches. How do the sounds affect the **mood** and meaning of each incantation?

2. How frightening is Hecate's description of what she is about to do? How effective is the **repetition** in the spirits' song and the **imagery** of the little spirit sitting on a cloud?

3. Plan where Hecate will enter and where the various chanting spirits will be. What kind of dancing might they do? Briefly **choreograph** their moves, creating and arranging a series of dance steps. What kind of vocal effects can you provide to make up for the lines' deficiencies in language and effect?

After you have **blocked** and rehearsed the scene, present it to another group or to half the class, and then watch and listen to another group's scene. As you listen to each other's readings, see if you can understand why scholars are so sure this scene is not Shakespeare's, and hypothesize how actual productions of *Macbeth* might handle this scene. Would you include it if you were producing the play? Why or why not?

Lesson 32
Analysis of Tone, Syntax

Lennox, speaking to another lord, here plays a **role** similar to that of the **chorus** in ancient Greek drama, standing apart and providing commentary on the action. Shakespeare's **choral character**, one person providing commentary, is also part of the play. Removed from the action, Lennox provides a perspective which may be seen as the norm: the point of view of the larger group --in this case, the people of Scotland:

> The gracious Duncan
> Was pitied of Macbeth: marry, he was dead;
> 5 And the right valiant Banquo walked too late,
> Whom you may say, if 't please you, Fleance killed,
> For Fleance fled: men must not walk too late.
> Who cannot want the thought how monstrous
> It was for Malcolm and for Donalbain
> 10 To kill their gracious father? Damnèd fact,
> How it did grieve Macbeth! Did he not straight
> In pious rage the two delinquents tear,
> That were the slaves of drink, and thralls of sleep?
> Was not that nobly done? Ay, and wisely too,
> 15 For 'twould have angered any heart alive
> To hear the men deny't. So that I say
> He has borne all things well, and I do think
> That had he Duncan's sons under his key—
> As, an't please heaven, he shall not—they should find
> 20 What 'twere to kill a father. So should Fleance. (3.6.3–20)

The unnamed lord to whom Lennox is speaking responds with news of the planned attack by the rightful king and Macduff's departure for England to seek the help of the English monarch. This **choral character** provides information about action that happens **offstage**, and then reassures Lennox about the future:

> we may again
> Give to our tables meat, sleep to our nights,
> Free from our feasts and banquets bloody knives,

Do faithful homage, and receive free honours,
All which we pine for now. (3.6.33–37)

Exercise A — Paraphrase the words of Lennox.

Exercise B — Describe in detail the **tone** taken by Lennox. What clue to **tone** are we given in line 19? What other clues are to be found in the **diction**? What purpose is served by introducing this point of view at the end of the third act?

Exercise C — Compare the **tone** of the unnamed lord's words with that of Lennox. Then describe the unusual **syntax**, and comment on its effect.

MACBETH

Lesson 33
Analysis of Irony, Figurative Language

Macbeth has demanded that the witches conjure their "masters."
He listens to the words of each apparition, but does not seem to
pay attention to what he sees, though their strange forms are surely
symbolic, suggesting something beyond themselves. Thus, he does not
understand the significance of three visions:

> FIRST APPARITION (an armed head):
> Macbeth, Macbeth, Macbeth, beware Macduff,
> Beware the Thane of Fife. Dismiss me. Enough. (4.1.87–88)

> SECOND APPARITION (a bloody child):
> Be bloody, bold, and resolute. Laugh to scorn
> The power of man, for none of woman born
> Shall harm Macbeth. (4.1.95–97)

> THIRD APPARITION (a child crowned, with a tree in his hand):
> Be lion-mettled, proud, and take no care
> Who chafes, who frets, or where conspirers are.
> Macbeth shall never vanquished be until
> Great Birnam Wood to high Dunsinane Hill
> Shall come against him. (4.1.106–110)

Exercise A — What do the three speeches suggest to Macbeth? If the
first is a warning, how would you describe the other two?

Exercise B — What does the armed head suggest to you about
Macduff's plans? The bloody child is an enigma to us as well
as to Macbeth, but as for the crowned child, what should we
recall (which Macbeth conveniently forgets) from the first of
the witches' prophecies? Does Macbeth consider the **equivocal**
nature of the word *until*?

On Your Feet X
Lesson 33

In a group of three or four members, practice reading the lines of the first three apparitions called forth by the witches: Act 4, Scene 1, lines 87–88, 95–97, and 106–110. Keep in mind that the fourth apparition is the long line of kings resembling Banquo. The first three prophecies are all riddles that hold the key to the play's outcome.

After a close reading of Lesson 33, try to convey a sense of warning and **foreboding** while also maintaining the mystery of the riddles. Discuss the following as you prepare to read the prophecies:

1. As Lesson 33 explains, the apparitions are **symbolic**. Prepare something you can hold—a drawing or **prop**—to convey the **symbolism** of each apparition. If possible, use the class time to create the drawing or **prop** for your reading; you also may find or create these at home.

2. Practice reading the apparitions' speeches using different pitches and sounds. Remember, the witches and these apparitions are other-worldly so you will want to practice voices that convey that supernatural sense.

3. One person in the group should read Macbeth's lines in response to each apparition after you have discussed Lesson 33, Exercise C. Discuss how you will show Macbeth's obliviousness to the witches' **equivocation**, and demonstrate within your group.

Present your readings of the scene to the class.

Lesson 34
Analysis of Metaphors

In this terrible scene, in which Ross tells Macduff about Macbeth's pitiless revenge against him, the **dialogue** gives us two views of manliness, that of Macduff and that of Malcolm, the rightful king:

> MALCOM   Let's make us medicines of our great revenge
> To cure this deadly grief.
> MACDUFF   He has no children. All my pretty ones?
> Did you say all? O hell-kite! All?
> What, all my pretty chickens and their dam
> At one fell swoop? (4.3.215–220)

The **dialogue** develops the **motif** of manliness:

> MALCOM   Dispute it like a man.
> MACDUFF   I shall do so,
> But I must also feel it as a man.
>
> . . . . .
>
> 230   MALCOLM   Be this the whetstone of your sword. Let grief
> Convert to anger: blunt not the heart, enrage it.
> MACDUFF   O, I could play the woman with mine eyes
> And braggart with my tongue! But gentle heavens
> Cut short all intermission. Front to front
> 235   Bring thou this fiend of Scotland and myself.
>
> . . . . .
>
> MALCOLM   This tune goes manly. (4.3.221–223, 230–235, 237)

Exercise A — Unpack the two **metaphors** in the first exchange. In what ways is the **vehicle** of each appropriate to the speaker?

Exercise B — Discuss these views of manliness. Which of the speakers is the more mature and complete person, in Shakespeare's view?

Exercise C — If Shakespeare plans to end the play with an act of **poetic justice** in which the good are rewarded and the evil punished, which of these two will kill Macbeth? Justify your choice.

On Your Feet XI
Lesson 34

In Lesson 34, you studied several of Macduff's and Malcolm's lines in response to the slaughter of Macduff's family. Work with a partner on the first six lines of dialogue you examined: 4.3.215–220. If you have time, include the remaining lines from Lesson 34: 4.3.221–223, 230–235, and 237.

Before reading the **dialogue**, discuss and practice the following:

1. In lines 213–216 Malcolm uses a **metaphor**, analyzed in Exercise A, to drive Macduff to take action. Decide which words in the **metaphor** need vocal emphasis to convey Malcolm's determination and urgency. What gestures and facial expressions might convey Malcolm's emotions as he speaks to Macduff?

2. Among the first stages of grief are shock and denial. Which words in lines 217–220 suggest such shock and denial in Macduff? Which words will you emphasize to convey this sense of disbelief? Practice this emphasis with your partner.

3. If you have time to prepare the rest of the **dialogue**, decide how vocal variation can help you convey the contrasting attitudes toward manliness in lines 4.3.221–223.

Present your scene to the class.

MACBETH

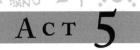
ACT 5

Lesson 35
Analysis of Prosody, Repetition

This scene is written in **prose**, ordinary speech, instead of verse. The sleepwalking Lady Macbeth is trying to wash imaginary blood from her hands:

30   Out, damned spot; out, I say. One, two,—why, then 'tis time to do't. Hell is murky. Fie, my lord, a soldier and afeard? What need we fear who knows it when none can call our power to account? Yet who would have thought the old man to have had so much blood in him?

. . . . .

Here's the smell of the blood still. All the perfumes of Arabia will not sweeten this little hand. O, O, O!

. . . . .

To bed, to bed. There's knocking at the gate. Come, come, come, come, give me your hand. What's done cannot be undone. To bed, to bed, to bed. (5.1.30–34, 42–43, 56–58)

Exercise A — Why is it appropriate that Lady Macbeth speak in **prose**? What is revealed about her state of mind by the **repetition** of words and phrases?

Exercise B — What moral truths has Lady Macbeth discovered since the night of Duncan's murder?

Exercise C — How does the discovery of these truths result in her madness?

On Your Feet XII

Lesson 35

Lady Macbeth's sleepwalking scene provides a fine opportunity for solo acting or a small group scene. On your own, practice only the **prose** lines 5.1.30–34, 42–43, and 56–58, as studied in Lesson 35. Another alternative is to work in groups of three on Act 5, Scene 1 in its entirety, with actors **cast** as Lady Macbeth, the doctor, and the waiting-gentlewoman. The challenge in this scene is to convey the deep despair and horror Lady Macbeth has repressed and which are evident in her subconscious.

Discuss and practice the following as you prepare the scene. If you are working on your own, you can still discuss these points with a partner:

1. How does Lady Macbeth move? How will her movements and facial expression convey the doctor's description that "her eyes are open" but "their sense are shut," as the waiting-gentlewoman observes in line 22? Show your partner how you will maintain the solemn **mood** of the scene while enacting Lady Macbeth's sleepwalking.

2. What does Lady Macbeth do with her hands? Show your partner how you will emphasize Lady Macbeth's agonized lines with her hand wringing. Be sure to include enough bodily tension in these actions to suggest the depth of Lady Macbeth's despair.

3. What will you have Lady Macbeth do with the taper she is carrying? Set it on a table? Crouch down and put it on the floor? Continue to hold it while going through the hand-washing motions?

4. Practice the **pacing** of Lady Macbeth's lines: Are they slow or fast? Where will you pause?

Practice the solo lines or scene aloud with your partner. Several volunteers will perform for the class or for half the class.

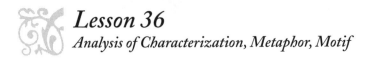

Lesson 36
Analysis of Characterization, Metaphor, Motif

Several thanes speak as **choral characters** before the armies attack
Macbeth's castle:

15   CAITHNESS   He cannot buckle his distempered cause
Within the belt of rule.

ANGUS   Now does he feel
His secret murders sticking on his hands.
Now minutely revolts upbraid his faith-breach.
Those he commands move only in command,

20   Nothing in love. Now does he feel his title
Hang loose upon him, like a giant's robe
Upon a dwarfish thief.

     . . . . . .

CAITHNESS   Meet we the medicine of the sickly weal.
And with him pour we in our country's purge,
Each drop of us.

LENNOX   Or so much as it needs

30   To dew the sovereign flower and drown the weeds. (5.2.15–22, 27–30)

Exercise A — Unpack the first **metaphor**. What is Macbeth's "cause"?
In what ways is the **vehicle** an appropriate one for Macbeth?

Exercise B — Explain the phrase "sticking on his hands." What
recent scene does this **metaphor** recall? Unpack the "giant's robe"
metaphor. Why is it appropriate? What has Macbeth stolen?

Exercise C — Explain "each drop of us" and the effect of its
hyperbole, or overstatement. What **motif** does it invoke?
The word *purge* expands on the first **metaphor**. Consider the
following definitions of the word: 1) to free from impurities by
cleansing; 2) to rid of sin, guilt, or defilement; 3) to rid a nation
of people considered undesirable; 4) in medicine, to cause
the emptying of the bowels. How does each of these apply to
Scotland's situation?

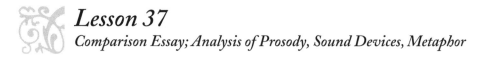

Lesson 37
Comparison Essay; Analysis of Prosody, Sound Devices, Metaphor

In *King John*, a history play which Shakespeare wrote seven years before *Macbeth*, Louis the Dauphin, in a state of mind similar to Macbeth's, says:

> There's nothing in this world can make me joy.
> Life is as tedious as a twice-told tale,
> Vexing the dull ear of a drowsy man;
> And bitter shame hath spoiled the sweet world's taste,
> That it yields naught but shame and bitterness. (KJ.3.4.107–111)

Macbeth, surrounded by avenging armies and having just heard that his wife has killed herself, says it this way:

> Tomorrow, and tomorrow, and tomorrow
> Creeps in this petty pace from day to day
> 20 To the last syllable of recorded time,
> And all our yesterdays have lighted fools
> The way to dusty death. Out, out, brief candle.
> Life's but a walking shadow, a poor player
> That struts and frets his hour upon the stage,
> 25 And then is heard no more. It is a tale
> Told by an idiot, full of sound and fury,
> Signifying nothing. (5.5.18–27)

Exercise A — Rather than simply counting the **stressed** syllables within a line, read each passage aloud several times, remembering not to pause except for punctuation. Decide which lines can be said quickly, and which must be said slowly.

Exercise B — Study the **sound devices** (especially the **metrical substitutions**) as well as the **metaphors** of the two passages. Gather evidence for an essay in which you demonstrate which of these statements is more compelling.

Exercise C — Decide, on the basis of your analysis, which of these passages is the more compelling, and in your essay explain why, citing evidence to support your points. State your thesis clearly and organize supporting evidence logically.

On Your Feet XIII
Lesson 37 Comparison Essay

You will be speaking Macbeth's "Tomorrow, and tomorrow, and tomorrow" **soliloquy** aloud several times before writing your comparison essay. This is an excellent passage to memorize or to perform for the class, too.

Discuss these preparatory questions and directions with a partner:

1. Look closely at the first complete sentence of the passage from "Tomorrow..." to the first period after "dusty death." What are the effect and implication of the **repetition** of "tomorrow"? How will you speak each "tomorrow" to highlight the **repetition**?

2. How do the words "creep" and "petty pace" in the second line support this interpretation? In practice, exaggerate the **consonance** in "cree**p**" and "**p**etty **p**ace," allowing this emphasis to slow down your reading rate.

3. How will your emphasis on the **alliteration** of "**d**usty **d**eath" convey the desolate life view of the entire passage? Practice only the first sentence. Memorize it by breaking it down into phrase groups.

4. What is the effect of the second sentence's brevity in contrast to the first long sentence? What is the candle? Practice and memorize the sentence with intensity and emotion.

5. As you look at the third sentence, speculate with your partner about how a shadow might "walk" and how a player on the stage would "strut" and "fret." Demonstrate each of these. Then practice and memorize the sentence, emphasizing "walking shadow," "struts," "frets," and "heard no more."

6. What kind of tale does an "idiot" tell? Practice and memorize this final, sorrowful sentence, emphasizing first the **alliteration** of "**t**ale **t**old" and then the words "idiot," "sound," "fury," and "nothing." You may wish to increase volume and intensity on "sound" and "fury."

Review the entire **soliloquy** and go over it a few more times for memorization. Having memorized the individual sentences, you will find mastering the entire passage easier. Present the passage to the class or a small group, delivering it with the emotional intensity Macbeth feels at this contemplative moment.

Lesson 38
Paraphrase, Analysis of Motif

Ross tells Siward about young Siward's death in the final battle:

5   ROSS   Your son, my lord, has paid a soldier's debt.
He only lived but till he was a man,
The which no sooner had his prowess confirmed
In the unshrinking station where he fought,
But like a man he died.
   SIWARD   Then he is dead?
10   ROSS   Ay, and brought off the field. Your cause of sorrow
Must not be measured by his worth, for then
It hath no end.
   SIWARD   Had he his hurts before?
   ROSS   Ay, on the front.
   SIWARD   Why then, God's soldier be he.
Had I as many sons as I have hairs
15   I would not wish them to a fairer death;
And so his knell is knolled. (5.11.5–16)

Exercise A — Paraphrase this **dialogue**.

Exercise B — Explain the several circumstances that make Siward call his son's death "fair."

Exercise C — Why is it appropriate that the play end with a final exploration of the manliness **motif**? What values have triumphed, and what can we infer are the values that have been defeated?

MACBETH

Accent The emphasis or **stress** given a syllable in pronouncing a word.

Alliteration The **repetition** of initial consonant sounds in nearby words.

Allusion A brief reference to a commonly known historical or literary figure, event, or object.

Ambiguity The intentional creation of multiple meanings. In a given context, a word may convey not only a denotation, but also **connotative** overtones of great richness and complexity.

Antithesis A rhetorical device contrasting words, clauses, sentences, or ideas, balancing one against the other in strong opposition. The contrast is often reinforced by the similar grammatical structure. See **Parallelism**.

Apostrophe A rhetorical device in which an absent or imaginary person or an abstraction is directly addressed as though present.

Aside A convention in Shakespeare's plays in which an actor directly addresses the audience, revealing his or her observations or emotions. The aside is not meant to be heard by the other characters on stage.

Assonance **Repetition** of vowel sounds in nearby words.

Atmosphere The prevailing **mood** of a scene or an entire play, often established by **scene-painting** describing the time of day, landscape, or weather. It infuses the action with an emotional aura, which influences the reader or viewer's expectations and attitudes.

Backstory The experience of a character or the circumstances of an event that happens before the play begins. Also called antecedent action.

Blank verse Unrhymed **iambic pentameter**, the form of verse most used in Shakespeare's plays.

Blocking The placing, grouping, and movement of actors on a stage.

Caesura	A pause in a line of verse created not by the **meter**, but by natural speaking rhythms, often coinciding with punctuation.
Cast	The group of actors who have roles in a play or the act of choosing the actors who will play each role.
Characterization	The creation, by means of speech, action, and gesture, of a sense of the moral, intellectual, and emotional qualities of the characters.
Choral character	A person who provides commentary on the action of the main characters, and who witnesses but stands apart from the action and provides a perspective which may be taken to be the norm (the point of view of the larger group).
Choreography	The art of creating and arranging a series of dance steps, often to music.
Chorus	In ancient Greek drama, groups of ordinary people who stand apart from, and provide commentary on, the action of the main characters.
Conflict	A struggle between characters in a drama or within a single character's mind that provides suspense and tension.
Connotation	Beyond denotation (the **literal** meaning of a word), **connotation** is the emotional implications and associations that a word carries. The context in which the word is found reveals its emotional coloring.
Consonance	**Repetition** of consonant sounds in nearby words.
Couplet	A unit of two consecutive lines of verse that ends with words that **rhyme**.
Cue	A signal, in word or action, used to prompt an actor's speech or entrance. Anticipating and picking up the cue quickly is an important skill for actors to master.
Dialogue	Conversation between two or more people.
Diction	The choice of individual words and patterns of words, diction helps differentiate among characters by social class and reveals emotional state. Patterns can be predominately positive or negative in **connotation**; concrete or abstract; **monosyllabic** or **polysyllabic**.

Disyllable	Word consisting of two syllables; also, **disyllabic**.
Downstage	Toward the audience.
Eleventh syllable	The common addition of an **unaccented** syllable at the end of a line of **blank verse.**
End rhyme	Rhyme used at the end of a line to echo the end of another line.
End-stopped line	A line of verse that ends when the grammatical unit ends.
Enjambed line	From the French meaning "a striding over," this term describes a line of verse in which the sense and grammatical construction continue on to the next line. The lack of completion creates pressure to move rapidly to the closure promised in the next line.
Equivocation	More than just than an **ambiguous** statement, an equivocal statement is deliberately open to two or more interpretations, and is often intended to mislead.
Figurative language	Figures of speech are any intentional departures from the normal meaning of words. The most commonly studied are **metaphors.**
Foil	A character who, through contrast, underscores the distinctive characteristics of another, often more important character.
Foot	In verse, a unit of **rhythm** created by a pattern of **accented** and **unaccented** syllables. The number of feet in a line constitutes its **line length.**
Foreshadowing	Preparation for later events in the plot, achieved by establishing **mood** or **atmosphere** or by revealing a fundamental and decisive character trait. Physical objects or **motifs** may also suggest later action.
Grounds	See *Metaphor.*
Hyperbole	**Figurative language** in which one says more than one means, overstating and exaggerating. It may be used to heighten another effect.
Iamb	A **foot** consisting of an **unaccented** syllable followed by an accented one. **Iambic meter** is the most common in English.

Iambic pentameter	A **meter** consisting of five **iambic** feet.
Imagery	A **literal** representation of a sensory experience or an object that can be known by the senses. **Imagery** is often visual, but may also be auditory, gustatory, olfactory, or tactile. It may be presented in patterns (e.g., all pleasant or all unpleasant, or all conjuring a particular sense).
Improvisation	The act of performing with little or no preparation; also, **improvise.**
In Character	Acting, moving, and speaking as the character would whose role you are playing.
Internal rhyme	Rhyme that occurs in the middle of a line.
Inversion of word order	A poetic device that involves changing the usual order of words.
Irony	A recognition of incongruities in event, situation, or structure in which reality differs from appearance. The operative word is "opposite." **Verbal irony** uses words that express the opposite of what is meant: praise implies blame or blame, praise. It is not to be confused with sarcasm, which is much more harsh and meant to be hurtful. **Situational irony** is a predicament or piece of luck, which is the opposite of what one would expect, given the circumstances. **Dramatic irony** occurs when a character reveals that he or she is unaware of something significant that the audience knows.
Line length	In verse, the terms for the number of feet in a line. We use a numerical prefix (one to eight) and the term "**meter**," meaning "measure": monometer, dimeter, trimeter, tetrameter, pentameter, hexameter, heptameter, and octameter.
Literal language	The factual sort of discourse that is without embellishment; the opposite of **figurative language**.
Loose sentence	A long sentence in which the subject and predicate are followed by many modifiers and subordinate ideas. These sentences tend to be rambling, with no phrase or clause receiving particular emphasis.

Metaphor	An implied comparison in which two unlike things are linked by a surprising similarity. Either thing or both may be unstated. The actual subject may be called the **tenor**, and the thing with which it is identified may be called the **vehicle**. The **grounds** are the aspects of the vehicle that apply to the tenor.
Meter	The repeated pattern of **stressed** and **unstressed** syllables in a line of verse. Of the four common **meters** in English, two are duple (two syllables in a **foot**) and two are triple (three syllables in a **foot**). Each kind of **foot** may be either rising (**accented** syllable at the end) or falling (**accented** syllable at the beginning). The Greek names for the **meters** are:

          iambic (duple rising: X /)

          trochaic (duple falling: / X)

          anapestic (triple rising: X X /)

          dactylic (triple falling: / X X)

Metonymy	A **metaphor** in which an associated word rather than the literal word is used, often a part to stand for the whole.
Metrical substitutions	Variations on the basic metrical pattern. The most common in the **iambic** line:
	substitute a **trochee** for an **iamb** at the beginning of a line for emphasis (initial inversion);
	use a **spondee** (two **accented** syllables) for emphasis;
	use a **pyrrhic** (two **unaccented** syllables) to speed the line;
	use a **rest** (the absence of the expected syllable or **foot**) to break the **rhythm** for some reason;
	add an **eleventh syllable** (**unaccented**) to the end of a line to move quickly to the next line;
	use a **caesura**, a break or pause in the line, variously placed and signaled by punctuation, which can affect meaning, **subtext**, and emphasis.
Monosyllable	A word of one syllable; also, **monosyllabic** (adjective form).
Mood	The **atmosphere** suggested in drama largely by the **diction** used by characters, which conjures an emotional response in the audience.

Motif	A dominant, repeated idea in a play, which may be expressed through **characterization**, verbal patterns, **metaphors**, or **imagery**. Such recurrent images, words, objects, or actions unify the work.
Multisyllable	A word with more than two syllables; also, **polysyllabic**.
Offstage action	Action that contributes to the plot, but is not witnessed by the audience.
Onomatopoeia	A Greek term for imitative sounds: the sound of the word suggests its meaning. Though sometimes the correspondence is merely vague association, the pattern of sound echoes the denotation of the word.
Pacing	The emphasis and speed of a given line as spoken by the actor. **Pacing** is affected not only by the actor's speed of delivery, but by the use of pauses, cue pickup, and facial and bodily responses.
Paradox	A rhetorical device that is a seemingly contradictory or absurd statement but is actually well founded, often with unexpected meaning, and always pointing to a truth.
Parallelism	A rhetorical device that presents similar ideas in a similar manner. One element of equal importance with another is similarly developed and phrased. In grammar, this is called parallel structure.
Pentameter	A line of verse with five **feet**.
Periodic sentence	This structure withholds the main clause or its predicate until the end of the sentence, forcing the reader to pay careful attention and await the ending, which is emphatic.
Personification	A kind of **metaphor** that endows ideas, abstractions, or inanimate objects with human form and capabilities.
Poetic justice	An ideal ending that rewards virtue and punishes vice.
Polysyllable	A word with more than two syllables; also, **multisyllabic**.
Props	**Stage properties**, such as a torch, a dagger, a crown, or a table set with plates and goblets, a bed, a throne.
Prose	Any speech which is not in lines of verse and which demonstrates no **rhythmic** pattern.

Prosody	Principles of versification, especially **meter**, **line length**, **rhyme** scheme, and form.
Pun	A play on words, either the different senses of the same word, or the similar sense or sound of different words.
Pyrrhic	A **foot** of two **unaccented** syllables, a frequent variant in **iambic** verse.
Repetition	A rhetorical device built into **rhyme** and **meter**, and also occurring in **parallelism** and in **diction**.
Rest	A pause created by a line of verse shorter than the prevailing pattern.
Rhetorical accent	An emphasis aside from the metrical pattern used to enhance meaning.
Rhyme	Sound correspondences often found at the ends of lines of verse (**end rhyme**) or within the line (**internal rhyme**). A **rhyme** scheme is the pattern of rhyming sounds, indicated by a letter of the alphabet for each similar sound.
Rhythm	The pattern or flow of sound created by the arrangement of **stressed** and **unstressed** syllables.
Role	The character portrayed by the actor.
Scansion	The system for describing the **rhythm** of verse by dividing lines into syllables and laying out the pattern of **accented** and **unaccented** syllables in order to discover the predominant **meter** in a poem.
Scene-painting	An actor's words, full of vivid **imagery**, which indicate details of the **setting**.
Set	Whatever is on stage in addition to the characters and their **props**.
Setting	The time of day, **atmosphere** of place, the weather, etc. in which the dramatic action takes place.
Simile	**Figurative** speech in which two unlike things are compared using "like" or "as." Both **tenor** and **vehicle** are named.
Soliloquy	A speech delivered when the speaker is alone on stage, meant to inform the audience of what is in the character's mind.

Sound devices	In addition to **meter** and **rhyme**, **sound devices** include **assonance, consonance, alliteration**, and **onomatopoeia**.
Spondee	A **foot** of verse containing two **accented** syllables.
Stage directions	Notes added to the text of a play to indicate to the actors the movement, attitude, manner, style, or quality of speech, character, or action. They may specify locations on stage from the perspective of the actor facing the audience: stage right / stage left; **downstage** (toward the audience) / **upstage** (away from the audience).
Stage properties	See *Props*.
Stress	The emphasis given a syllable in pronouncing a word; an **accent**.
Subtext	The underlying personality or motivation of a dramatic character implied in the script and interpreted by the actor in performance.
Symbol	An image with another layer of meaning; something that is itself and also stands for something else. A **symbol** combines the **literal** and sensuous qualities of an image with an abstract aspect, suggesting complex meanings.
Syntax	The arrangement of words within a sentence. **Syntax** includes sentence length and complexity; the variety and pattern of the sentence's form; inversion of natural word order; unusual juxtaposition; **repetition; parallelism**; use of active or passive voice; level of discourse; order, including emphatic or subordinate position of elements.
Tenor	See *Metaphor*.
Tone	The character's attitude as conveyed through **diction**, especially word **connotation**.
Trochee	A **foot** of verse in which an **accented** syllable is followed by an **unaccented** one.
Upstage	Away from the audience (near the back wall of the stage).
Vehicle	See *Metaphor*.